Welfare

OPPOSING VIEWPOINTS®

Welfare

OPPOSING VIEWPOINTS®

Other Books of Related Interest

Welfare

OPPOSING VIEWPOINTS®

James Haley, *Book Editor*

Daniel Leone, *President*
Bonnie Szumski, *Publisher*
Scott Barbour, *Managing Editor*

OPPOSING VIEWPOINTS® SERIES

GREENHAVEN PRESS®

THOMSON
GALE

San Diego • Detroit • New York • San Francisco • Cleveland
New Haven, Conn. • Waterville, Maine • London • Munich

THOMSON

GALE

LIBRARY OF CONGRESS CATALOGING-IN-PUBLICATION DATA

Welfare / by James Haley, book editor.
    p. cm. — (Opposing viewpoints series)
    Includes bibliographical references.
    ISBN 0-7377-1246-5 (lib) — ISBN 0-7377-1245-7 (pbk)
        1. Public welfare—United States—Juvenile literature. [1. Public welfare.]
    I. Haley, James, 1968– . II. Opposing viewpoints series (Unnumbered).
    HV91 .W467 2003
    361.6'0973—dc21
                                                                        2002000380

Printed in the United States of America

"Congress shall make no law...abridging the freedom of speech, or of the press."

First Amendment to the U.S. Constitution

The basic foundation of our democracy is the First Amendment guarantee of freedom of expression. The Opposing Viewpoints Series is dedicated to the concept of this basic freedom and the idea that it is more important to practice it than to enshrine it.

Contents

Why Consider Opposing Viewpoints?

"The only way in which a human being can make some approach to knowing the whole of a subject is by hearing what can be said about it by persons of every variety of opinion and studying all modes in which it can be looked at by every character of mind. No wise man ever acquired his wisdom in any mode but this."

John Stuart Mill

In our media-intensive culture it is not difficult to find differing opinions. Thousands of newspapers and magazines and dozens of radio and television talk shows resound with differing points of view. The difficulty lies in deciding which opinion to agree with and which "experts" seem the most credible. The more inundated we become with differing opinions and claims, the more essential it is to hone critical reading and thinking skills to evaluate these ideas. Opposing Viewpoints books address this problem directly by presenting stimulating debates that can be used to enhance and teach these skills. The varied opinions contained in each book examine many different aspects of a single issue. While examining these conveniently edited opposing views, readers can develop critical thinking skills such as the ability to compare and contrast authors' credibility, facts, argumentation styles, use of persuasive techniques, and other stylistic tools. In short, the Opposing Viewpoints Series is an ideal way to attain the higher-level thinking and reading skills so essential in a culture of diverse and contradictory opinions.

In addition to providing a tool for critical thinking, Opposing Viewpoints books challenge readers to question their own strongly held opinions and assumptions. Most people form their opinions on the basis of upbringing, peer pressure, and personal, cultural, or professional bias. By reading carefully balanced opposing views, readers must directly confront new ideas as well as the opinions of those with whom they disagree. This is not to simplistically argue that everyone who reads opposing views will—or should—change his or her opinion. Instead, the series enhances readers' understanding of their own views by encouraging confrontation with opposing ideas. Careful examination of others' views can lead to the readers' understanding of the logical inconsistencies in their own opinions, perspective on why they hold an opinion, and the consideration of the possibility that their opinion requires further evaluation.

Evaluating Other Opinions

To ensure that this type of examination occurs, Opposing Viewpoints books present all types of opinions. Prominent spokespeople on different sides of each issue as well as well-known professionals from many disciplines challenge the reader. An additional goal of the series is to provide a forum for other, less known, or even unpopular viewpoints. The opinion of an ordinary person who has had to make the decision to cut off life support from a terminally ill relative, for example, may be just as valuable and provide just as much insight as a medical ethicist's professional opinion. The editors have two additional purposes in including these less known views. One, the editors encourage readers to respect others' opinions—even when not enhanced by professional credibility. It is only by reading or listening to and objectively evaluating others' ideas that one can determine whether they are worthy of consideration. Two, the inclusion of such viewpoints encourages the important critical thinking skill of objectively evaluating an author's credentials and bias. This evaluation will illuminate an author's reasons for taking a particular stance on an issue and will aid in readers' evaluation of the author's ideas.

It is our hope that these books will give readers a deeper understanding of the issues debated and an appreciation of the complexity of even seemingly simple issues when good and honest people disagree. This awareness is particularly important in a democratic society such as ours in which people enter into public debate to determine the common good. Those with whom one disagrees should not be regarded as enemies but rather as people whose views deserve careful examination and may shed light on one's own.

Thomas Jefferson once said that "difference of opinion leads to inquiry, and inquiry to truth." Jefferson, a broadly educated man, argued that "if a nation expects to be ignorant and free . . . it expects what never was and never will be." As individuals and as a nation, it is imperative that we consider the opinions of others and examine them with skill and discernment. The Opposing Viewpoints Series is intended to help readers achieve this goal.

David L. Bender and Bruno Leone,
Founders

Greenhaven Press anthologies primarily consist of previously published material taken from a variety of sources, including periodicals, books, scholarly journals, newspapers, government documents, and position papers from private and public organizations. These original sources are often edited for length and to ensure their accessibility for a young adult audience. The anthology editors also change the original titles of these works in order to clearly present the main thesis of each viewpoint and to explicitly indicate the opinion presented in the viewpoint. These alterations are made in consideration of both the reading and comprehension levels of a young adult audience. Every effort is made to ensure that Greenhaven Press accurately reflects the original intent of the authors included in this anthology.

Introduction

"We do indeed need to end welfare—but as poor single mothers experience it, not as middle-class moralizers imagine it."

—Gwendolyn Mink, 1998

"The success of welfare reform demonstrates that failed liberal policies . . . need not be passively accepted as inevitable features of modern life."

—Ramesh Ponnuru, 2001

While campaigning for the presidency in 1992, former president Bill Clinton promised to "end welfare as we know it." Clinton was responding to public pressure to reform the program of public aid to the poor, known simply as "welfare," which by the early 1990s had developed a reputation as being wasteful and ineffective. In some ways, Clinton's vision of welfare, a vision that emphasized work instead of dependency on the government, was quite different from the program that originated with Aid to Dependent Children (ADC), created by the Social Security Act of 1935. Michael Kelley, a researcher with the libertarian Cato Institute, describes ADC as a means-tested program with low-income eligibility requirements that was intended as a "national system of support for families in which the fathers were dead, disabled, or absent." Poor mothers were expected to stay at home with their children and did not have to perform outside work in exchange for benefits. In the intervening years, ADC was renamed Aid to Families with Dependent Children (AFDC), and eligibility requirements were expanded to include two-parent families in which the primary breadwinner was unemployed.

Congress began a major overhaul of welfare beginning in 1994, and two years later, President Clinton followed through on his campaign pledge and signed legislation replacing AFDC with Temporary Assistance for Needy Families (TANF). Under TANF, the federal government delivers money, in the form of block grants, to states, thereby allowing states greater flexibility and authority in administering their welfare programs. This new program represented a changed vision of welfare's purpose. Rather than a program of long-term assistance for the needy, welfare was officially considered a short-term program to help people become self-supporting. Heads of households are expected to find work within two years of receiving benefits, and families face a lifetime limit of five years of cash assistance.

No matter how welfare programs have been structured, they have always been unpopular with the public at large. While the work requirements instituted as part of welfare reform may have tempered public criticism to a degree, the majority of Americans continue to regard welfare recipients—by and large unwed or divorced single mothers—with equal parts scorn and impatience. In part, this is because work is not a prerequisite for collecting welfare benefits. In other words, welfare is not a "work-tested" program. Observes conservative commentator Mickey Kaus, "Most government benefit programs have been 'work-tested' since their inception. . . . Unemployment compensation is conditioned on prior participation in the labor force. Social Security pensions go only to citizens who've worked a sufficient number of 'quarters.'. . . It's no accident that these big programs are work-tested; otherwise they wouldn't have been popular enough to get passed by Congress. The two great exceptions to the general work test, AFDC ('welfare') and food stamps, are exceptions that 'prove the rule.'. . . AFDC only came into being as an 'entitlement' through a backdoor process that involved a minimum of democratic approval by Congress and a maximum of intervention by the federal bureaucracy and the courts." Critics such as Kaus maintain that in exempting a large group of Americans from the work test, the government has created a protected class of citizens who are, based on lack of income, entitled to cash payments denied workers who pay their fair share of taxes.

Public resentment of welfare also has a strong basis in the program's perceived diminution of the work ethic, the idea that hard work will lead to a better life. According to Virginia Postrel, editor-at-large of *Reason* magazine, "Americans deeply resent both the welfare system and its beneficiaries . . . resentment that is turning a culture of self-reliance and individualism into a culture of victimhood and nosy animosity. . . . Welfare's defenders often disparage work—especially low-paid and manual work—and the people who value it. They imply that anyone who does such work is a victim or a sucker." Many Americans feel insulted and threatened by welfare's perceived disparagement of the work ethic. As a result, much of the public is in agreement with critics who see welfare as promoting out-of-wedlock childbearing, dependency on the government, and drug abuse, and are angered by reports of fraud and abuse of the system perpetrated by some recipients.

Still, the public support for Congress' latest attempt to reform welfare is testimony that no matter how cynical Americans may have become regarding welfare, a majority still feel an obligation to help poor families. This desire to help the poor while upholding cherished American values of hard work, individualism, and community is the central conflict facing reformers as they grapple with the future of welfare and its reform. Anne Marie Cammisa, author of *From Rhetoric to Reform: Welfare Policy in American Politics*, describes how the welfare debate places Americans in an ideological bind, forcing a compromise between competing philosophies of individualism and community. Explains Cammisa, "If a person isn't elderly, has no physical problems, and yet doesn't work and has no money, many of us believe that he or she should learn to take care of himself or herself, that society doesn't have an obligation when individuals refuse to help themselves. But what if that person has children? Should the value of individualism include them, or should they be taken care of under the value of community? . . . Under what circumstances should the community feel an obligation to help? These are some of the difficult questions that welfare reform must answer." How the welfare system should be changed to minimize this conflict of values is debated and discussed in *Welfare: Opposing Viewpoints*. Chapters include: Does Welfare Encourage Dependence? Is Abuse of the Welfare System a Serious Problem? Can Private Efforts Replace the Welfare System? How Should Welfare Be Reformed?

CHAPTER 1

Does Welfare Encourage Dependence?

Chapter Preface

From the mid-1960s to the early 1970s, the number of Americans on welfare grew from 4.3 million to close to 10 million, according to the Cato Institute, a libertarian think tank. Peter Edelman, the author of *Searching for America's Heart*, maintains that the rising welfare population during this period was caused by the loss of jobs in the inner city, as manufacturing operations left New York, Chicago, and Philadelphia for less expensive regions of the country and the world. According to Edelman, the changing economic situation in inner cities coincided with growing sentiment among the poor that they had a "right" to welfare and should not be abandoned to an unreliable economy and the whims of government generosity. Explains Edelman, "Inspired by the civil rights movement and community-action activism, welfare recipients organized to demand fair treatment at the welfare office. . . . [In addition,] the Supreme Court . . . responded positively to welfare recipients in a number of landmark cases. . . . By the end of the sixties welfare had become a real statutory right instead of simply a program by which local bureaucrats could help those they liked." Defenders of the system maintained that so long as the government ignored the structural problem of unemployment and the ill effects of poverty, it was obligated to uphold the poor's right to welfare benefits.

Critics of the welfare system argue that the rapidly swelling welfare rolls had less to do with economic conditions than with the poor exercising their newly won rights to welfare benefits. The strong economy and low unemployment rate during that period support their assertion that the poor were shunning plentiful jobs in favor of government handouts. The welfare rights movement eliminated the stigma associated with accepting public assistance, and long-term dependency on the government replaced responsible behavior with illegitimacy, drug abuse, and crime, according to the critics. Echoing the contention of many conservative commentators, the editors of the *Washington Times* asserted in 1996 that welfare dependency had doubled Washington, D.C.'s teen birth rate over a ten-year period. They argued that it would be "unconscionable" to allow such dependency to continue.

With the passage of the 1996 welfare reform law, Congress formally ended welfare as a guaranteed cash entitlement to poor families. The law imposes work requirements on recipients and limits them to five years of assistance during a lifetime. Supporters of welfare rights maintain that the law caters to conservative fears regarding welfare dependency and seeks to punish poor mothers who bear children out of wedlock. The emphasis on welfare dependency has obscured the more substantive issue of the government ignoring its obligation to assist the poor to self-sufficiency, according to liberal reformers. Whether the government has such an obligation and whether such help can be administered without continuing the harmful aspects of dependency is examined and debated by the authors in the following chapter.

"When [government] gives money to the unemployed, . . . it undermines the social disapproval of idle dependency."

The High Value of Welfare Benefits Keeps the Poor on Welfare

James L. Payne

In the following viewpoint, James L. Payne contends that generous welfare benefits offer recipients a greater financial reward than full-time work, enticing many single mothers onto the welfare rolls. According to Payne, welfare payments promote idleness and dependency by undermining the social disapproval and painful consequences of dysfunctional behaviors like drug addiction and unwed childbearing. As a result, social norms have shifted to the point where welfare recipients are no longer ashamed of relying on the government to support their irresponsible lifestyles. Payne is the author of *Overcoming Welfare: Expecting More from the Poor—and from Ourselves.*

As you read, consider the following questions:

1. In Payne's opinion, how does the growth of the food stamp program illustrate the "aggravation principle" of sympathetic giving?
2. How much would a job have to pay a welfare recipient before her earnings from work exceeded her welfare earnings, according to the author?
3. In the author's opinion, what role does social disapproval play in deterring people from engaging in behavior that leads to dependency?

S ocial reformers have often been dismayed by the way problems of poverty seem to grow *after* they begin programs of assistance. It seems profoundly unfair that their efforts should be rewarded not by a solution to neediness but by more of it. The history of the federal government's food stamp program illustrates the pattern.

Uncontrolled Growth of Assistance

After operating it as a pilot program in the early 1960s, the Kennedy administration turned food stamps into a permanent program in 1963. The object was to supply the poor with vouchers that they could use to pay their grocery bills. Secretary of Agriculture Orville L. Freeman came to the House Agriculture Committee to explain the administration's expectations about the eventual size and scope of the program. "We estimate," he said in his prepared testimony, "that, with a continuation of current economic conditions, a stamp program could be expanded over a period of years to about 4 million needy people." The eventual yearly cost of the fully established program was expected to be $119 million.

As time passed, the number of food stamp recipients grew and costs escalated, yet the goal of "ending hunger" kept receding. The paradox was highlighted in 1988 when Congress reexamined the program. It was then costing $12 billion, one hundred times what was first estimated, and the number of recipients had grown to 20 million, five times the number of hungry originally thought to exist. Instead of finding that the problem of hunger had been solved by the vast expansion of this and many other food aid programs, Congress discovered a "hunger emergency." So it passed the Emergency Hunger Relief Act, which further expanded food stamp benefits. By 1995 spending for food stamps had increased to $26 billion and the average monthly number of recipients was 28 million, yet food policy specialists declared that "some 13 million children under age 12 in the United States are hungry or at risk of hunger."

What happened to invalidate Secretary Freeman's original estimates? We might understand the numbers if the United States had suffered a series of famines or a military invasion. But the economy was expanding during this period, and welfare experts expected prosperity to reduce the need for assistance. In 1957 the director of the American Public Welfare Association, Loula Dunn, was so confident of the beneficial effect of economic growth that she predicted, "We can expect the volume of public assistance cases to decrease in the future." By rights, the number of people unable to buy food for themselves should have been going down.

The Aggravation Principle

The paradox illustrates the aggravation principle of sympathetic giving: giving prompted by misfortune tends to increase the incidence of misfortune. Thus, a program designed to feed people who can't seem to feed themselves results in even more people who can't seem to feed themselves.

The aggravation principle lies at the core of problems with government assistance programs. For some two hundred years, it has loomed over welfare policy—alternately ignored, then painfully recognized, then ignored again. The challenge is not so much to explain the aggravation principle, for it is virtually a truism, but to identify the errors in perception that cause people to disregard it. Only by understanding these errors can we hope to avoid another two hundred years of stop-start anguish on the welfare front. . . .

"Work or Starve"

Between 1850 and 1870, the United States increased welfare benefits—and then discovered that poverty had not been alleviated, but had increased. According to an account of the period by the charity historian Marvin Olasky, the new largesse was prompted by the emergence of a naive idealism about human nature in certain journalistic and literary circles. Horace Greeley, founder and editor of the *New York Tribune*, was one of the leaders of this native socialist movement. He favored having the state redistribute income by taxing the wealthy and giving their money to the less well-off. He did not worry that the dole might weaken the motivation of the poor because he was convinced that human beings are naturally industrious by nature. "The heart of man is not depraved," said Greeley. "His passions do not prompt to wrong doing, and do not therefore by their action, produce evil."

Greeley and many other journalists, novelists, and academics agitated for, and achieved, a considerable increase in cash assistance by local governments in many cities. The result was that relief rolls climbed. In New York City, for example, the number on "temporary" relief rose from 12,000 in 1840 to 174,000 in 1860. By 1870 one-tenth of the population was receiving doles from the city.

Instead of producing a new breed of enlightened poor, these giveaways seemed only to result in more begging and in abuse and corruption of the welfare system. Public opinion swung against the dole, and government relief programs were curtailed or eliminated in most cities in the 1870s and 1880s. Many of the budding socialists learned a valuable lesson about human motivation. Greeley himself made a dramatic turnabout. By 1869 he was complaining that "the beggars of New York are at once very numerous and remarkably impudent." He judged nine-tenths of them to be "shiftless vagabonds" and concluded that the best way to respond to a beggar was to refuse aid. "Make up a square issue—'Work or starve!'—and he is quite likely to choose work."

These decades taught a generation of American charity workers the perils of sympathetic giving. Even official bodies got the message. The New York State Board of Charities carefully explained why a government cash relief program was unsound: "When persons, naturally idle and improvident, have experienced for a few months the convenience of existing upon the labor of others, they are very likely to resort to this means of living as often and as continuously as possible."

The Economic Effects of Sympathetic Giving

The modern welfare state has repeated the nineteenth century's experience with the aggravation principle. Welfare programs and benefits have been substantially increased over the past half-century, although not necessarily in each program. The overall trend, however, compared with 1950, is higher benefits, more generous eligibility criteria, and many more overlapping programs.

When the benefits of welfare programs are combined, they can add up to an extremely attractive economic package. To document this point, three researchers from the Cato Institute calculated the value of six of the main assistance programs in 1995: Aid to Families with Dependent Children (AFDC), food stamps, Medicaid, housing assistance, nutrition assistance, and energy assistance. The yearly value of this welfare package, for recipients who took advantage of all six programs, ranged from $27,736 in Hawaii to $13,033 in Mississippi (see Table 1).

To assess how these benefits compared to working a forty-hour week, being taxed, and taking no welfare benefits, the researchers calculated the hourly wage a worker would have to be paid to achieve the welfare level of "take-home pay." In every state, welfare paid much more than the minimum wage of $4.25 per hour. In the state with the median level of benefits, welfare paid $9.18 per hour. In other words, a welfare recipient would have to find a job paying more than $9.18 an hour before his earnings from work exceeded his earnings from welfare.

Table 1: Wage Equivalents of Welfare Benefits (Dollars)

	Full Package			AFDC, Food Stamps, Medicaid		
	Total Benefits	Yearly Income Equiv.	Hourly Wage Equiv.	Total Benefits	Yearly Income Equiv.	Hourly Wage Equiv.
High	27,736	36,100	17	19,071	21,300	10
Median	17,780	19,100	9	11,797	10,100	5
Low	13,033	11,500	6	7,353	6,100	3

David Kelley, *A Life of One's Own*, 1998.

This study has been criticized because it assumed that recipients benefited from all six welfare programs. However, studies based on actual welfare recipients confirm the general point. Douglas Besharov of the American Enterprise Institute found that in 1992 the average unwed mother on welfare obtained a total of $17,434 a year in benefits, while the same woman working full-time (and also receiving some welfare benefits) ended up with $15,583. The result is a "welfare trap" that makes dependency economically attractive.

Welcome to Welfare

The increase in the economic benefits of welfare over the past half-century has attracted a growing number of people to the welfare rolls. At any one time, some 16 percent of U.S. households are drawing assistance from one or more welfare programs. The proportion of the population utilizing welfare is even higher than this, since many recipients follow a pattern of "serial dependency": they leave a welfare program but later return to it—or go on another.

Many studies have documented the point that benefits from welfare programs—unemployment benefits, food stamps, AFDC—reduce work effort. One notable set of findings came out of the studies of guaranteed income in the 1970s. In extremely sophisticated experiments, particularly in Denver and Seattle, poverty-level families were split into two groups: one group received additional income support according to their level of need, and the other group were not given additional support. The families with the income assistance showed significantly lower levels of work effort.

In the typical case, welfare payments promote dysfunctional behavior not so much by making the behavior positively attractive, but by making it *less unattractive* than it would otherwise be. Defenders of the welfare system often miss this point. They cite, for example, the unhappy situation of an indigent teen with an illegitimate child, even with welfare. "Since life as an indigent teen mother is so difficult," they argue, "how can anybody say that welfare payments attract women to this lifestyle?"

But welfare payments have their negative effect, not by making indigent childbearing attractive, but simply by lessening its unattractiveness. Normally, to have a child without being married to a steady wage earner would produce an extremely painful, even tragic, result for the mother. What welfare payments do is lessen the painful penalties associated with indigent unwed childbearing—which is thus increased, as many studies have shown.

The Social Effects of Sympathetic Giving

Economic motives are not the only ones shaping recipients' responses to welfare programs. Human beings are attracted to—and repelled by—activities and roles not only because of material rewards but also because of the social approval and disapproval associated with them. We care what others think about us, and we usually avoid activities that are frowned upon, even if they promise an economic reward.

Social disapproval can play a large role in deterring people from engaging in behavior that leads to neediness. If society frowns on drunkenness, or drug addiction, or unwed childbearing, possible social rejection helps dissuade people from such behavior. Unfortunately, sympathetic giving weakens the social disapproval of harmful behavior by appearing to endorse it.

How should parents react to the pregnancy of one of their unwed teenage daughters? Of course they want to help her, but agreeing to take care of her and her child sends the message that they don't disapprove of unwed teen childbearing. Hence, the other daughters are less likely to expect parental disapproval if they get pregnant—and they are thus more likely to do so. Again, the way out of the dilemma is some arrangement of expectant giving that lets the parents help without seeming to approve of the misbehavior. They can insist that the daughter marry the father of the child, or give the baby up for adoption, or work part-time to help support the baby.

Government Authority and Social Norms

Sympathetic giving, then, communicates social approval of the lifestyle that led to misfortune. This point especially applies to government programs. Government is the source of law and authority in society, and therefore its assistance programs broadly influence social norms. When it gives money to the unemployed, including those who are idle and dependent, it undermines the social disapproval of idle dependency. When it gives benefits to couples who have more children than they can support, it undermines the social stigma of having families larger than one can take care of.

Most school systems today provide prenatal care for pregnant unwed students, as well as day care after their babies arrive. While these benefits have an economic value to the mothers, their main effect is not economic but social. Such programs undermine the stigma of unwed teen pregnancy. Until fairly recently, girls who got "in trouble" were whispered about—and expelled from school. Seeing this social disapproval, other girls made a great effort to avoid pregnancy. Today programs like free day care for student mothers make unwed teen pregnancy seem almost normal—not "trouble" at all, but a viable option intentionally chosen by girls in certain subcultures.

Analyzing government welfare programs only in economic terms is a mistake. By reducing the stigma attached to dysfunctional behavior, their main effect over the years has been social. The arrival of a check every month for a certain type of problem can seem like a natural way to "earn" a living after a while. Even nonrecipients have become habituated. One notices, for example, that workers in most nonprofit charities see federal assistance programs—housing subsidies, SSI, food stamps—as a legitimate long-term means of support for their clients. Government assistance is such a natural part of the landscape that getting people signed up for it seems like a method of self-help!

The Proudly Dependent

In Lake Providence, Louisiana, Rosie Watson collects nine welfare checks, which give her and her family a total, tax-free yearly income of $46,716. Beginning her welfare career as an unwed mother on AFDC, Watson turned to the supplemental security income program for disabilities in 1978. She eventually got all of her seven children enrolled for various types of mental disabilities. Her common-law husband was declared disabled on grounds of obesity. In her own case, she was turned down five times because doctors agreed she was not disabled. (One commented, "Patient is determined to become a ward of the government.") Finally, on appeal, an administrative law judge declared her eligible on grounds of "stress."

How do we know all these confidential details? So proud was she of her entrepreneurial tenacity that Rosie eagerly told her story to the *Baltimore Sun* reporters John O'Donnell and Jim Haner. In an earlier day, welfare recipients would have been embarrassed about their dependency. But now, decades of government cash payments for idle people have undermined the stigma associated with being unproductive and dependent. "I've got nothing to hide," Rosie told reporters. "SSI has done a lot for our family. We're not able to work, and it's the best income."

> *"Unless the typical unskilled or semiskilled single mother finds an unusually well-paying job . . . she cannot work her way from dependency to self-sufficiency."*

A Lack of Opportunities Keeps the Poor on Welfare

Kathryn Edin and Laura Lein

Kathryn Edin and Laura Lein interviewed 214 welfare-reliant women in the early 1990s about the economic circumstances that led them to choose welfare benefits over work. In the following viewpoint, the authors maintain that the minimum wage jobs available to unskilled single mothers leave them no better off financially than remaining or signing onto the welfare rolls. According to Edin and Lein, low-wage work does not offer the training, experience, or education that would facilitate advancement into higher paying jobs and lacks the medical coverage available to families under the welfare system. For these reasons, many mothers who would prefer the self-sufficiency of regular work resign themselves to dependency on welfare. Edin and Lein are the authors of *Making Ends Meet: How Single Mothers Survive Welfare and Low-Wage Work*.

As you read, consider the following questions:

1. What percentage of welfare mothers interviewed by the authors had worked within the past five years?
2. According to the authors, why did most of the mothers they interviewed believe that taking a low-wage job might make them worse off than remaining on welfare?

Excerpted from *Making Ends Meet: How Single Mothers Survive Welfare and Low-Wage Work*, by Kathryn Edin and Laura Lein (New York: Russell Sage Foundation, 1997). Copyright © 1997 by Russell Sage Foundation. Reprinted with permission.

S ocial scientists have little direct evidence of how single mothers themselves view the incentives and disincentives associated with welfare or work. Do mothers make their decisions using a cost-benefit approach? How do government policies influence these decisions? Could government policies do more to encourage work? In our 1992 interviews, we spoke to welfare-reliant mothers at length about their economic circumstances and how they chose to deal with them. This viewpoint records what mothers actually said about the incentives and disincentives of welfare and work in the early 1990s. These first-hand accounts of the factors that influenced their welfare/work decisions provide important insights to those who seek to formulate welfare policies that are effective in moving mothers from welfare to work for good.

The Welfare vs. Work Dilemma

Our data lend a good deal of support to the idea that mothers choose between welfare and work by weighing the costs and benefits of each. Most of the welfare-reliant mothers we interviewed had an accurate view of the benefits they would lose by going to work—although they did not always know the exact dollar amount—and they made reasonable assessments of how much they would need to earn to offset the added costs of work. Mothers' views of the incentives and disincentives of each, however, were quite different from those assumed by many social scientists, including [conservative Charles] Murray. For poor single mothers, the welfare/work choice was not merely a problem of maximizing income or consumption. Rather, each woman's choice was set against a backdrop of survival and serious potential material hardship. The mothers with whom we spoke were less interested in maximizing consumption than in minimizing the risk of economic disaster. . . .

We interviewed 214 welfare-reliant women, most of whom said that their decision regarding whether to leave welfare was predicated on their past labor-market experiences. These experiences shaped their estimates of their current job prospects. Contrary to popular rhetoric, mothers did not choose welfare because of a *lack* of work experience or because they were ignorant of their job options. Most of the welfare-reliant mothers we interviewed had held a job in the formal sector of the labor market in the past: 83 percent had some work experience and 65 percent had worked within the last five years. National data, though not directly comparable, suggest an even higher rate of labor-market participation; 60 percent of all welfare recipients surveyed by the Panel Study of Income Dynamics (PSID) had worked during the previous two years. On average, our welfare recipients had accumulated 5.6 years of work experience before their current spell on welfare.

Lessons from Low-Wage Work Experience

Their experience in the low-wage labor market taught these mothers several lessons about their likely job prospects. First, returning to the kinds of jobs they had held in the past would not make them better off—either financially or emotionally—than they were on welfare. Indeed, this was precisely why most mothers were receiving welfare rather than working. Second, most mothers believed that taking a low-wage job might well make them *worse* off, because the job might vanish and they might be without any income for a time, since it took months for the welfare department to redetermine welfare eligibility and cut the first check. Consequently, working might put them and their children at risk of serious hardship. Third, no matter how long they stayed at a job and no matter how diligently they worked, jobs in what some called "the five-dollar-an-hour ghetto" seldom led to better jobs over time. Fourth, since job clubs and other components of the federal Job Opportunities and Basic Skills training program (JOBS) were designed to place mothers in the types of jobs they held in the past, they saw little reason to participate in these programs: JOBS training programs added little to mothers' earning power. Finally, mothers took noneconomic as well as economic factors into account when deciding between welfare and work. Although most mothers felt that accepting welfare carried a social stigma, they also feared that work—and the time they would have to spend away from home—could jeopardize the safety and well-being of their children.

Given these realities, it was surprising to us that most

mothers still had plans to leave welfare for work. Some planned to delay leaving welfare until their children were older and the cost of working was lower. Others . . . planned to use their time on welfare to improve their skills so they could get a better job when they reentered the labor force. In the long run, the goal of most mothers was to earn enough to eliminate the need for any government welfare program and to minimize their dependence on family, friends, boyfriends, side-jobs, and agencies. . . .

Half the [214] . . . welfare-reliant [mothers] . . . were engaged in some form of work (formal or informal) to make ends meet. Most had also worked at a job in the formal sector at some time in the past, and the vast majority planned to do so in the future. Indeed, they all knew that they would have to work in due course, since their children would eventually reach adulthood, making the family ineligible for welfare. Only a tiny portion had no concrete plans to work in the formal sector.

Calculating Costs and Benefits

When welfare-reliant mothers thought about welfare and work, the vast majority calculated not only how their prospective wages would compare with their cash welfare and food stamp benefits but how much they would lose in housing subsidies and other means-tested benefits. They also calculated how much more they would have to spend on child care, medical care, transportation, and suitable work clothing if they were to take a job. This mother's comment was typical:

> One day, I sat down and figured out the balance of everything that I got on welfare [including fuel assistance and Medicaid] and everything that I [earn] and have to spend working. And you know what? You're definitely better off on welfare! I mean absolutely every woman wants to work. I always want to work, but it's hard.

Because the costs and benefits associated with leaving welfare for work were constantly on their minds, many of the women we interviewed could do these calculations off the top of their heads, and some were able to show us the backs of envelopes and scraps of notebook paper on which they had scribbled such calculations in the last few weeks.

Although respondents' estimates were seldom exact, most mothers were able to describe their prospective loss in benefits and potential increase in expenses. They were also able to calculate how holding a regular job would affect their ability to supplement their income in various ways. . . . In addition, mothers considered a variety of noneconomic "costs" of working: whether full-time work would leave them enough time to be competent parents and whether they could manage to keep their children safe from the potentially lethal effects of their neighborhoods. Mothers' concerns about their children's welfare were often as important as purely economic gains or losses in their decisions. . . .

Apart from believing that working was a financial wash, women also felt they would gain little self-respect from the minimum-wage jobs they could get with their current skills. Nearly all of our welfare-reliant respondents said they would feel better about themselves if they could make it without welfare, but this boost to their self-esteem seemed to depend on a working life that offered somewhat higher wages and better prospects for advancement than most of the jobs they thought they could get with their current skills and job experience.

Risking the Future

The cost-benefit calculations that mothers made about leaving welfare for work were colored by the economic and social contexts of these women's lives. As we mentioned earlier, the mothers we interviewed had to weigh the utility of work against the real possibility that a subsequent layoff or reduction in hours could lead to serious material hardship. The jobs these mothers could get were among the least reliable in the U.S. economy. Typically, they demanded work at irregular hours, did not guarantee how many hours a worker would be able to work in a given week, and were subject to frequent layoffs. Nowhere was this more true than in the fast food industry. When we asked "What's the problem with working at a place like a fast food restaurant?" one welfare-reliant Chicago mother with eight years of experience in fast food restaurants told us,

They work you really hard and you can't even get full-time

hours. Those jobs are for the kids. I wouldn't go back because there would be no money. There is not even enough money for the teenagers, let alone for an adult supporting a family. It's for teenagers I feel, and I'm beyond that.

Fast food chains typically impose unpredictable schedules on workers, sending them home when business is slow. As a result, women could not predict how many hours they would be able to work. One mother recounted,

> Like I was supposed to work until 11:00 today. They turned around and sent me home at 9:30 in the morning. I get so mad. They make you slave and [then] they don't give you regular hours.

Even worse, if the job failed, it usually took several months to get their benefits going again, leaving these mothers with no source of legal income in the interim. A Chicago respondent expressed the frustration with the lag in benefits this way:

> [Because of the way the system is set up] it's just really hard to get off of [welfare]. When you go get a job, you lose everything, just about. For every nickel you make, they take a dime from you. [I have been] on and off welfare. Like when I [tried] working at a nursing home, I was making $4.50 an hour [and] they felt like I ma[de] too much money. Then they cut me off. And I just couldn't make ends meet with $4.50 an hour, because I was paying for day care too. So I [had] to quit my job to get back on it. It took me forever to get back on, and meanwhile I had to starve and beg from friends. . . .

To aggravate matters, a large proportion of those respondents who stayed at one job in order to work their way up were eventually laid off. Peter Gottschalk and Sheldon Danziger found that women working in low-wage jobs were three times more prone to job layoffs than other workers. One might expect that unemployment insurance would provide a safety net for such workers, but this is seldom the case. The percentage of job losers who collected unemployment declined throughout the 1980s. At the end of the decade, less than one in three jobless workers reported receiving unemployment benefits (about 34 percent were eligible), and those in the low-wage sector were the least likely to have coverage. This is presumably because an increasing proportion of Americans are working at jobs that are not covered by these benefits. [In 1994,] Roberta Spalter-Roth, Heidi

Hartmann, and Beverly Burr found that only 11 percent of welfare recipients with substantial work hours were eligible for unemployment insurance.

Dead-End Jobs

The vast majority of those who had worked also found that hard work rarely led to anything better. Their past jobs had seldom produced the type of "human capital" (training, experience, or education) that they could parlay into better jobs. Nor did they produce the "social capital" (professional contacts and links with other jobs or employers) that might improve their career prospects, since they worked with other women in equally low level jobs. In short, these women were unable to build careers; if they chose to work, they were much more likely to move from one dead-end job to another. Thus, women learned that the kinds of jobs available to them were not avenues to success or even to bare-bones self-sufficiency; they were dead ends.

One respondent from the low-wage worker group, an African American woman in her late thirties with a high school diploma, had spent twenty years working for a large

Table 1: Plans of 214 Welfare-Reliant Mothers

	Number	Percent
	214	*100%*
No plans to leave welfare for work	29	14
Permanently disabled	10	5
Plan to marry	5	2
Situation too unstable	4	2
Prefer to combine welfare with unreported work	10	5
Plan to leave welfare for work	185	86
Plan to leave now	27	13
Plan to leave in the future	158	73
Child's age only	16	7
Need for training only	13	6
Child's age and need for training	105	49
Temporary disability	24	11

Authors' calculations using Edin and Lein survival strategies data.

regional grocery chain. She worked the first fifteen years as a cashier, earning the minimum wage. In 1986, management promoted her to the service counter and raised her hourly wage from $3.35 to $4.00 an hour. In 1991, after five years in her new position, she had worked her way up to $5 an hour, the highest wage she had ever received. She had virtually never been late or taken a sick day, and her boss told her she was one of his most competent employees, yet her hourly salary over the past twenty years had risen by a total of $1.65. . . .

Most mothers told us they had originally entered the labor market with high hopes. They believed that if they could manage to stay at one job long enough or, alternatively, use each job as a stepping stone to a better one, they could make ends meet through work. After a few years in the low-wage job sector, they saw that instead of achieving their goals they were getting further and further behind in their bills. Not surprisingly, mothers concluded that the future they were building through low-wage work was a house of cards. . . .

Earnings Problems

National data echo these mothers' experiences. First, a large body of research has shown that low-wage work does not pay a living or family wage. Charles Michalopoulos and Irwin Garfinkel estimate that workers with demographic profiles resembling those of typical welfare-reliant mothers could expect to earn only $5.15 an hour (in 1991 dollars) if they left welfare for work. Diana Pearce's analysis of PSID data also shows that for 70 percent of welfare-reliant mothers in the 1980s, spells of low-wage employment left them no better off than they had been before. The kinds of jobs that are available to these women more often end up being "chutes" not ladders.

Second, there is growing evidence that low-wage jobs provide little or no access to better future jobs. In their book *Working but Poor*, Sar Levitan and Isaac Shapiro write that,

> Evidence of mobility among the working poor should not obscure the serious and enduring labor-market problems that this group faces. Their prospects may be better than those of the non-working poor, but many of the working poor have

long-term earnings problems. More than any other indicator, including demographic characteristics such as education or race, the best predictor of future status in a low-wage job is whether or not a worker is currently in a low-wage job. A core group of the working poor remains impoverished for many years. . . . [Furthermore], the deteriorating conditions of the 1980s may have exacerbated the labor-market difficulties of the working poor and extended the duration of their poverty spells.

Unless the typical unskilled or semiskilled single mother finds an unusually well-paying job or has medical benefits, a child care subsidy, and very low housing and transportation costs, she cannot work her way from dependency to self-sufficiency. Despite this reality, many single mothers remained committed to the work ethic and tried to leave welfare again and again. Many had such varied job histories that their employment records sounded like the newspaper's "help wanted" advertisements. Most mothers had moved from one job to another, always looking for some slight advantage—more hours, a better shift, a lower copayment on a health plan, more convenient transportation, less strenuous manual labor, or less monotonous work—without substantially improving their earnings over the long term. . . .

The vast majority of our sample—86 percent (or 185 mothers)—was planning to leave welfare for work (see Table 1). This is not surprising: survey researchers have repeatedly found highly favorable attitudes toward work among the welfare poor. Yet only 13 percent of all those in the sample who wanted to work (twenty-seven mothers) believed they could afford to leave welfare at the time we interviewed them. Seventy-three percent of the total (158 mothers) said that, while they both wanted and planned to leave welfare for work, they could not afford to take the kind of job they thought they could get at the time.

"By removing the economic consequences of an out-of-wedlock birth, welfare has removed a major incentive to avoid unmarried pregnancy."

Welfare Causes an Increase in Out-of-Wedlock Births

Michael Tanner and David B. Kopel

In the following viewpoint, Michael Tanner and David B. Kopel contend that welfare payments have removed a major incentive for poor women to avoid unmarried pregnancy by cushioning the economic hardship of out-of-wedlock child-bearing. According to Tanner and Kopel, surveys of inner-city teenage girls reveal carefree attitudes toward having babies out of wedlock, attributable to the availability of welfare. In addition, studies have demonstrated a link between an increase in welfare benefits and a corresponding increase in births to unmarried low-income women, as cited by the authors. Tanner is the author of *The End of Welfare: Fighting Poverty in the Civil Society*. Kopel is research director of the Independence Institute, a conservative think tank.

As you read, consider the following questions:
1. By what percentage have out-of-wedlock births increased since 1960, according to the authors?
2. In the authors' opinion, how does welfare remove the consequences of an out-of-wedlock birth in the eyes of teenagers?
3. How has the availability of welfare undermined marriage in cases where the father has limited employment prospects?

Excerpted from "Welfare Reform: Next Steps for Colorado," by Michael Tanner and David B. Kopel, *Independence Institute Issue Paper*, January 14, 1997. Copyright © 1997 by the Independence Institute. Reprinted with permission.

Perhaps the gravest social challenge facing America today is the huge decline in the number of children living with two parents. In 1960, more than 80 percent of children lived with their mother and father. An additional 6.7 percent lived with either their mother or father and a stepparent. By 1990, only 57.7 percent of children lived with two biological parents, with an additional 11.3 percent living with a stepparent. The majority—over sixty percent—of all children will not live with both parents until age eighteen. As few as 6 percent of black children born in 1980 will live with both parents until age eighteen, some researchers project.

Skyrocketing Out-of-Wedlock Births

The most important component behind the rise in single-parent families is births to unmarried women. . . . Out-of-wedlock births have increased by more than 400 percent since 1960. In 1960, only 5.3 percent of all births were out-of-wedlock. Among whites, only 2.3 percent were out-of-wedlock, while the out-of-wedlock rate among blacks was 23 percent. By 1990, 28 percent of all births were out-of-wedlock. The rate among whites had increased to an alarming 21 percent, and among blacks had skyrocketed to an astonishing 65.2 percent. In ten major American cities in 1991, over half of all births were illegitimate. In some urban neighborhoods, 80 percent of all births are illegitimate. . . .

The concern over the increased rate of out-of-wedlock births is not a question of private morality. If Murphy Brown [a television character criticized by then–Vice President Dan Quayle in 1992] was typical of unwed mothers, objections would be far more muted. However, only 4 percent of out-of-wedlock births to white mothers are to women with a college degree, while 82 percent of such births are to women with a high school education or less. Women with incomes of $75,000 or more contribute only 1 percent of white out-of-wedlock births, while women with family incomes under $20,000 contribute 69 percent.

Having a child out of wedlock often means many decades or even a lifetime in poverty for both mother and child. Approximately 30 percent of all welfare recipients start on welfare because they have an out-of-wedlock birth. The trend is even worse among teenage mothers. Half of all unwed teen mothers go on welfare within one year of the birth of their first child; 77 percent are on welfare within five years of the child's birth.

Moreover, once on welfare, many of these women find it very difficult to get off. While the average length of time spent on welfare is relatively short, generally two years or less (since many people use welfare as it was intended, as a temporary safety net), 65 percent of persons enrolled in the program at any one time have been on the program for eight years or longer. Single mothers make up the largest portion of these long-term recipients. Single women average 9.33 years on welfare and make up 39.3 percent of all recipients who are on welfare for ten years or longer.

Effects on Children

The non-economic consequences of out-of-wedlock births are equally stark. There is strong evidence that the absence of a father increases the probability that a child will use drugs and engage in criminal activity. According to one study, children raised in single-parent families are one-third more likely to exhibit anti-social behavior. Yet another study indicated that, holding other variables constant, black children from single-parent households are twice as likely to commit crimes as black children from a family where the father is present. The likelihood of criminal activity triples if he lives in a neighborhood with a high concentration of other single-parent families. Nearly 70 percent of juveniles in state reform institutions come from fatherless homes.

Compared to children from two-parent households, children from single-parent homes perform significantly worse in school. They are three times more likely to fail and repeat a year of school, are more likely to be late, have disciplinary problems in school, and perform poorly on standardized tests, even when studies control for differences in family income. They are twice as likely to drop out of school altogether.

Children from single-parent families are two to three times more likely to experience mental illness and other psychological disorders. Nearly 80 percent of children admitted to psychiatric hospitals come from single-parent homes.

There is also evidence that child abuse occurs more frequently in single-parent homes.

And the problem perpetuates itself. For example, white women raised in single-parent households are 164 percent more likely to bear children out-of-wedlock themselves. Moreover, children raised in a single-parent family are three times more likely to become welfare recipients as an adult.

This is not to criticize any particular single mother. Millions of single mothers do tremendous jobs of raising healthy, happy, and successful children against difficult odds. Still, children growing up in single-parent homes are clearly at a higher risk, particularly when they have no contact with their father, even when very young. Obviously, therefore, a society that purports to care about children should discourage out-of-wedlock births as a matter of policy.

Linking Out-of-Wedlock Births to the Welfare System

Perhaps no issue of welfare reform has been as hotly debated as the link between the availability of welfare and out-of-wedlock births. Since Charles Murray raised the issue in *Losing Ground*, experts have lined up on both sides of the issue. . . .

Of course, the large majority of women who receive welfare do not get pregnant just to get welfare benefits. It is also true that a wide array of other social factors has contributed to the growth in out-of-wedlock births. But, by removing the economic consequences of an out-of-wedlock birth, welfare has removed a major incentive to avoid unmarried pregnancy, or to allow a child born out-of-wedlock to be adopted by a married couple. A teenager looking around at her friends and neighbors is liable to see several who have given birth out-of-wedlock. When she sees that they have suffered few visible consequences (the very real consequences of such behavior are often not immediately apparent), she is less inclined to modify her own behavior to prevent pregnancy, and less inclined to give the child to an adoptive family if she does become pregnant.

Proof of this can be found in a study by Professor Ellen Freeman of the University of Pennsylvania, who surveyed black, never-pregnant females age 17 or younger. Only 40 percent of those surveyed said that they thought becoming pregnant in the next year "would make their situation worse." Likewise, a study by Professor Laurie Schwab Zabin for the *Journal of Research on Adolescence* found that: "in a sample of inner-city black teens presenting for pregnancy tests, we reported that more than 31 percent of those who elected to carry their pregnancy to term told us, before their pregnancy was diagnosed, that they believed a baby would present a problem. . . ." In other words, 69 percent either did not believe having a baby out-of-wedlock would present a problem or were unsure.

Asay. © 1997 by Creators Syndicate, Inc. Reprinted with permission.

As Murray explains, "The evil of the modern welfare state is not that it bribes women to have babies—wanting to have babies is natural—but that it enables women to bear children without the natural social restraints."

Until teenage girls, particularly those living in relative poverty, can be made to see real consequences from pregnancy, it will be impossible to gain control over the problem of out-of-wedlock births. By disguising those consequences, welfare makes it easier for these girls to make the decisions that will lead to unwed motherhood.

Reviewing the Evidence

During the New Deal, President Roosevelt's Secretary of Labor, Frances Perkins, argued against extending federal benefits to unwed mothers because she believed that subsidizing illegitimacy would lead to the breakdown of the family. Ms. Perkins was right.

A review of recent studies provides increasing evidence that welfare *does* contribute to rising rates of out-of-wedlock births:

In a paper presented to the National Academy of Sciences, Marl Rosenzweig of the University of Pennsylvania reported that a review of data from the National Longitudinal Survey of Youth showed that a 10 percent increase in welfare benefits resulted in a 12 percent increase in births to unmarried low-income women ages 14 to 22.

A study by June O'Neill and Anne Hill for the U.S. Department of Health and Human Services found that an increase in monthly welfare benefits led to an increase in out-of-wedlock births. Holding constant a wide range of variables, including income, education, and urban vs. suburban setting, the study found that a 50 percent increase in the value of Aid to Families with Dependent Children (AFDC) and food stamp payments led to a 43 percent increase in the number of out-of-wedlock births.

Research by Shelley Lundberg and Robert Plotnick of the University of Washington showed that an increase in welfare benefits of $200 per month per family increased the rate of out-of-wedlock births among teenagers by 150 percent.

Professor C.R. Winegarden of the University of Toledo concluded that half the increase in the out-of-wedlock birth rate since 1965 was due to the perverse incentives of welfare.

Mikhail Bernstam of the Hoover Institution found that in cities with large black populations, the birthrate among single teenage women increased 10 percent for each 10 percent increase in welfare benefits.

In a 1989 study, Martha Ozawa found a statistically significant correlation between AFDC payments and the illegitimacy rate for adolescents.

A 1993 study in the *Journal of Marriage* by Mark Fosset and Jill Kiecolt found a substantial and consistent relationship between the size of public assistance payments and out-of-wedlock births among black women ages 20–24.

In all, there have been 16 major studies of the link between welfare and out-of-wedlock births; 13 of them found a statistically significant correlation.

In addition, focusing solely on the out-of-wedlock birthrate may actually understate the problem. In the past, women who gave birth out of wedlock frequently married the father of their child following the birth. Marvin Olasky, for example, estimates that as many as 85 percent of unmarried pregnant women in the 1950s ultimately married the fathers of their children. Therefore, while technically an out-of-wedlock birth, the child was still likely to grow up in an intact two-parent family.

However, the increasing availability of welfare may have made such marriages unattractive for many unwed mothers. If the father is unskilled and has no high-paying employment prospects, a welfare check may seem a preferable alternative. Studies indicate that young mothers and pregnant women are less likely to marry the fathers of their children in states with higher welfare benefits. In addition, research by Robert Hutchins of Cornell University shows that a 10 percent increase in AFDC benefits leads to an 8 percent decrease in the marriage rate of single mothers. Discouraging marriage tends to perpetuate poverty, since the leading way for women to move off welfare is to get married and stay married.

Welfare also appears to have a modest but significant impact on increasing abandonment and divorce, and decreasing remarriage after divorce.

"The links between welfare and family structure begin to crumble on close examination."

Welfare Does Not Cause an Increase in Out-of-Wedlock Births

Michael B. Katz

In debating the 1996 welfare reform law, many political leaders argued that guaranteed welfare payments under the Aid to Families with Dependent Children (AFDC) program offered women an economic incentive to have children, remain unmarried, and shun employment. As a result, AFDC was replaced by a program emphasizing time limits and personal responsibility. Michael B. Katz asserts in the following viewpoint that the easy availability of welfare payments was not to blame for the rise in out-of-wedlock births and dependency on public assistance. According to the author, limited job prospects for inner-city men and inadequate education have influenced whether poor, unwed women will have children far more than the inducement of welfare benefits. Katz is the Stanley I. Sheerr Professor of History at the University of Pennsylvania.

As you read, consider the following questions:
1. By how much did the number of children in the average welfare family decline from 1969 to 1993, according to the author?
2. In Katz's opinion, how did the structure of the AFDC welfare program undermine independence and self-support?

Rising alarm shared by both Republicans and Democrats at out-of-wedlock births and the consequences of dependency provoked the 1990s assault on Aid to Families with Dependent Children (AFDC). The numbers were alarmingly high: in 1995, 56 percent of black children lived in single-parent families, compared with 33 percent of Hispanics and 21 percent of whites. In 1994, 70 percent of black children were born outside marriage. This large number of single-parent families kept poverty rates high because about half of them were poor. The "new politics of poverty," observed political scientist Lawrence Mead, was about dependence, not money. Welfare experts Mary Jo Bane and David Ellwood wrote, "It is hard to miss the profound shift in emphasis and tone in poverty discussions over the past ten to fifteen years. A decade or two ago, the academic debate and to a large degree the popular debate were often focused on matters of adequacy, labor supply responses, tax rate, and opportunity. Now 'dependency' is the current preoccupation."

Blaming Welfare for Out-of-Wedlock Births

In the 1980s, Charles Murray's book *Losing Ground* proved the most influential conservative attack on AFDC. Murray argued that the well-meaning but misguided extension of social benefits during the Great Society years had fueled the rise of single-parent families, out-of-wedlock births, and dependence. Although social scientists thoroughly discredited Murray's book by exposing its shoddy statistics and fallacious arguments, their writing did little, if anything, to dislodge it as a respected source among conservatives or to lessen its use by politicians. In the 1990s, Robert Rector played something of the same role as Murray, although without a major book. Rector, along with William F. Lauber, argued that "the welfare system has paid for non-work and non-marriage and has achieved massive increases in both. By undermining the work ethic and rewarding illegitimacy, the welfare system insidiously generates its own clientele. . . . Welfare bribes individuals into courses of behavior which in the long run are self-defeating to the individual, harmful to children, and increasingly a threat to society." Welfare's worst result was "its corrosive effect on family structure, driving up illegitimacy, which in turn is a powerful factor contributing to other social problems." It also fueled "long-term inter-generational dependence," thereby "trapping many families in a repeating cycle of debilitating and self-destructive behavior."

Not jobs, wages, or globalization, but the collapse of family threatened America's future, and its major source was welfare. The answer lay in the total reconstruction of welfare policy to enforce morals, support marriage, and push women into the labor force. The stakes were very high. The future of America hung on the ability of social policy to turn around the behavior of young black and Hispanic women. Pennsylvania's Senator Rick Santorum, who helped design the Republican position on welfare, said most Republicans believed welfare "is the number-one societal problem, that it's at the root of the disintegration of families in the inner city, the social decay we have seen in the last 20 years. What we have to stop doing is guaranteeing people failure. These programs have done nothing but keep people poor."

Responding to Conservative Critics

The links between welfare and family structure begin to crumble on close examination. Like Murray, Rector and Lauber do not explain why AFDC rolls climbed as benefits declined. If young women responded to incentives, the rolls should have grown smaller. They also ignore the falling fertility of black women—the steady reduction in the number of children in an average AFDC family, from 4 in 1969 to 2.8 in 1993. And other than the inducement of "welfare" benefits, they offer no explanation for declining marriage rates and rising out-of-wedlock births among black women—low wages and the poor job prospects of African American men, for instance, play no role in conservative explanations.

Indeed, the timing of demographic trends undermined the attempt to pin the blame for these trends on AFDC. Unmarried mothers often needed public assistance to survive, and the increase in their numbers drove up the AFDC rolls. However, the availability of AFDC is not the reason why the number of out-of-wedlock births and single-parent families increased. In fact, after the recession of the early 1990s began to ease, AFDC rolls started to decline. Among blacks, births to unmarried women, the number of one-parent families with a never-married mother, and the number of children living with one parent all also moved downward from their peak. Other parts of the conservative criticism likewise disintegrated under close analysis. Studies found that surprisingly small numbers of women who grew up in welfare-dependent families were themselves dependent, and three of four supported by public assistance had not received it as children. Although daughters (but not sons) growing up in AFDC-dependent households were somewhat more likely than others to turn to AFDC themselves, by itself the correlation proved nothing about causation. Many other factors, such as parents' education, poverty, the quality of schools, and the impact of neighborhood could have influenced the outcome. In the welfare debates of the 1990s, conservative accounts of research simply misrepresented the evidence. James Q. Wilson, professor of management and public policy at the University of California, Los Angeles, dismissed the argument that abolishing AFDC would reduce out-of-wedlock births as "in large measure based on untested assumptions, ideological posturing and perverse priorities. . . . It is, at best, an informed guess."

Elusive Independence

Very large numbers who left the AFDC rolls were poor in the following year—a result of low wages. Not surprisingly, within two years, more than half the women who had left AFDC to take a job were back on the rolls. This "churning" of the AFDC rolls—the frequent movement on and off—showed that poor families try to find ways to help themselves. By and large, they did not want to remain dependent on government, and their personal histories described an intermittently successful search for an elusive independence. Many, of course, did not leave; they composed the core of long-term recipients—the majority of women on AFDC at any one time—incorrectly believed typical of women assisted by AFDC. For them, AFDC indeed had become a way of life.

The program's own structure, in fact, undermined independence and self-support more than the bad example set

Average Family Size, Selected Years, 1969–1992

Year	Average Number of Persons in AFDC Household (includes parent(s) as well as children)
1969	4.0
1973	3.6
1975	3.2
1979	3.0
1983	3.0
1986	3.0
1988	3.0
1990	2.9
1992	2.9

Anne Marie Cammisa, *From Rhetoric to Reform? Welfare Policy in American Politics*, 1998.

by parents or the generosity of AFDC's benefits. Eligibility rules defeated attempts to save modest amounts of money or keep a reliable car to drive to work. The rules allowing recipients to keep some of their earnings, virtually eliminated during the Reagan years, removed incentives to supplement AFDC with work. The threatened loss of medical insurance built risk into the exchange of AFDC for a low-wage job, and without subsidies for child care, employment often was impossible. These structural impediments in AFDC increasingly appeared irrational to both conservatives and liberals, and state waivers focused on modifying many of them. Indeed, governors, tired of asking Washington for waivers, demanded further devolution and chafed at persisting federal controls—at the need, as governors put it, to beg Washington to ask permission to experiment. Representative Gerald Solomon of New York told the House, "We have heard testimony on this floor from State after State that [in] the waiver process . . . thoughtful and experimental governors must troop to Washington DC, hat in hand, and request permission to reform low-income programs at home. The waiver request is then subject to endless debate by bureaucrats and subject to negotiation and even change by the Federal departments involved."

Many ordinary Americans objected to welfare for other

reasons. As they worked harder for less pay, many resented what they believed was the free ride offered by welfare, and many working mothers, now the majority, found it hard to understand why "welfare mothers" should not be compelled to juggle the same burden of work and child care as they did every day. The most important component in Americans' intense dislike of welfare, reports political scientist Martin Gilens, was the "widespread belief that most welfare recipients would rather sit home and collect benefits than work hard to support themselves." Representative John Kasich of Ohio reminded his colleagues in the House of the "cynicism" felt about AFDC by "the folks who get up and go to work every day for a living. . . . Those mothers and fathers who have had to struggle for an entire lifetime to make ends meet, they have never asked for Food Stamps, they have never asked for welfare, they have never asked for housing, and they are struggling. . . . These people were becoming cynical, they were being poisoned in regard to this system, and they were demanding change."

To many, "welfare" became a code word for race, and the "welfare problem" signified the rising number of young, unmarried black or Hispanic mothers on the rolls. In 1994, people of color composed a majority, 63 percent, of AFDC recipients—a number that had increased solidly during the past decade. The proportion was much higher in conservative, "antiwelfare" southern states. The share of black AFDC recipients was 75 percent in Alabama, 74 percent in Georgia, and 83 percent in Mississippi. In older cities, it was very high as well—for instance, 97 percent in Washington, D.C. The color of welfare intensified the gulf between its clients and the white working poor and reinforced the conservative attack on AFDC. By placing responsibility for out-of-wedlock births and single-parent families on AFDC, conservatives helped discredit government policy and reinforced the belief that government is the source of social problems, not their solution. By offering up a convenient scapegoat for widespread anxieties about economic insecurity and fears of downward mobility, they helped construct an image of the undeserving poor that fractured the potential for political unity among low-income Americans.

Periodical Bibliography

The following articles have been selected to supplement the diverse views presented in this chapter.

Michael Barone	"Changing Minds," *U.S. News & World Report*, July 30, 2001.
Christopher D. Cook	"Welfare Rights Redux," *Z Magazine*, January 1998.
Patricia Donovan	"The 'Illegitimacy Bonus' and State Efforts to Reduce Out-of-Wedlock Births," *Family Planning Perspectives*, March/April 1999.
Christina Duff	"Why a Welfare 'Success Story' May Go Back on the Dole," *Wall Street Journal*, June 15, 1999.
Frank Field	"Welfare Dependency and Economic Opportunity," *Family Matters*, Spring/Summer 1999.
Melissa Healy	"More Ex-Welfare Recipients Are Working but Still Poor," *Los Angeles Times*, May 28, 1999.
Raymond Hernandez	"Most Dropped from Welfare Don't Get Jobs," *New York Times*, March 23, 1998.
Toby Herr and Suzanne Wagner	"Learning to Live Without the Welfare Check," *New York Times*, March 4, 2000.
Tamar Levin	"Cut Down on Out-of-Wedlock Births, Win Cash," *New York Times*, September 24, 2000.
New Republic	"Not So Welfare," April 13, 1998.
Michael M. Phillips	"Welfare's Urban Poor Need a Lift—to Suburban Jobs," *Wall Street Journal*, June 12, 1997.
Robert Rector	"Not So Poor: The Luxury of American Poverty," *National Review*, October 25, 1999.
Robert Rector	"Welfare Reform and the Decline of Dependence," Heritage Foundation, September 9, 1999. www.heritage.org.
Ben J. Wattenberg	"Linking Illegitimacy to Welfare," *AEI On the Issues*, August 1998. www.aei.org.
Karl Zinsmeister, Stephen Moore, and Karlyn Bowman	"Is America Turning a Corner?" *American Enterprise*, January 1999.

CHAPTER 2

Is Abuse of the Welfare System a Serious Problem?

Chapter Preface

In 1997, the *New York Times* ran an article on the Southside neighborhood in Brooklyn, where half the population of 27,000 received welfare benefits. To a casual observer, such a high percentage of people on welfare would seem to indicate that a dismal local economy had driven many families onto the welfare rolls. But in 1997, New York City was undergoing its greatest period of economic expansion since the 1960s, and unemployment was declining rapidly in many areas of the city. Instead of destitution, the reporter, Joe Sexton, uncovered a culture where widespread abuse of the welfare system had become a way of life. Women routinely collected welfare benefits while working on the side and living illegally with boyfriends or husbands in subsidized housing intended for those with lower incomes. Rosemarie Pizarro, a single mother interviewed by Sexton, described the general culture of welfare abuse: "Their answer to their own dishonesty has always been roughly the same: Everybody else is doing it. . . . There are third-generation and fourth-generation recipients in our buildings. That is why it is so impossible for them to believe it is coming to an end."

Exploitation of the welfare system will soon come to an end for many Southside residents, if it has not already done so. Following passage of the 1996 welfare reform law, New York City began to force recipients to work for their benefits, a requirement officials hoped would deter those planning to cheat the system with unreported jobs from joining the welfare rolls. In addition, the 1996 law limits families to a maximum of five years on public assistance, ending the tendency to spend a lifetime manipulating the welfare system.

As the effects of the welfare reform law play out, there is little disagreement among participants in the welfare debate that fraud has been a commonplace feature of the welfare system. Where critics disagree is over where to place the blame for welfare fraud. To taxpayers leery of seeing their hard-earned dollars wasted on manipulation and deceit, the blame falls squarely on welfare mothers and "deadbeat dads" who father children and expect others to pick up the tab. Responsible behavior would preclude the need for welfare in the first place, but fraud makes welfare all the more untenable to its many critics. As Tom Ridge, the former governor of Pennsylvania, observes, "When someone's down on their luck, we'll do all that we can to help them get back on their feet. . . . That generosity is what makes welfare fraud such a heinous crime. . . . It's a crime against our trust and generosity." Studies suggest that the majority of welfare mothers are supplementing their benefits with unreported jobs and contributions from boyfriends and relatives, betraying the public trust that recipients are truly in need of assistance. To critics, the welfare system should become ever more vigilant in screening out fraudulent applicants.

Observers sympathetic to the plight of poor single mothers are less concerned with the fact that abuse is occurring than with the forces driving the abuse. They maintain that poor single mothers often find that the welfare system discourages self-sufficiency. The benefits are too low to support a family, yet reporting supplementary income results in a sanctioning or loss of benefits. Even child support payments are of little use to welfare mothers, since the payments go directly to states as compensation for welfare benefits. Consequently, welfare mothers are caught in a real financial bind that leads to unreported jobs and illegal living arrangements out of necessity. According to some reformers, welfare should grant mothers more flexibility to accumulate personal savings, even if that means granting full benefits while allowing full-time work.

The elimination of fraud and abuse is an essential component in restoring public faith in the welfare system. The viewpoints in the following chapter examine what causes abuse within the welfare system and what measures can be undertaken to prevent it.

| "*[Government] needs to prove that it has the will to prevent the massive cheating [of the welfare system] that has been going on for generations.*"

Welfare Fraud Is Widespread

James L. Payne

James L. Payne is the author of *Overcoming Welfare: Expecting More from the Poor—and from Ourselves*. He asserts in the following viewpoint that welfare recipients are cheating the government out of billions of dollars each year through the abuse of welfare programs. Many welfare recipients have income through full- or part-time jobs or from boyfriends and family members that makes them ineligible for public assistance. Payne contends that recipients illegally sell food stamps in order to buy beer, cigarettes, and drugs. In the author's opinion, welfare officials ignore welfare fraud out of fear that a perception of waste will lead to funding cutbacks that could jeopardize their own jobs.

As you read, consider the following questions:

1. In the author's opinion, why is there pressure on welfare officials to keep adding more welfare clients to their programs?
2. How many of the twenty-five welfare recipients interviewed for a 1988 study on welfare fraud had unreported income, as cited by Payne?
3. As reported by the author, what did John Gardiner and Theodore Lyman conclude about the limited fraud control efforts of welfare agencies?

In cataloging the pressures that push government aid systems into the handout mode, we need to note a factor common to all institutionalized giving: the separation of donors from recipients. When we directly give our own resources to those in need, we don't want our aid to create an open-ended dependency because that would drain us financially. So we look for ways to help that will make the recipient independent and let us end our aid. Hence, personal systems of assistance have a bias toward expectant giving, toward helping the needy stand on their own feet.

In an institutional system of assistance, with workers being paid to help the needy, the incentives run in the opposite direction. Welfare officials are not dispensing their personal funds; they are giving away other people's money. They do not suffer financially from open-ended giving. For them, the financial pinch comes when the money *stops* being given away, when the program is shrunk or closed down and their jobs disappear. Thus, the self-interest of workers and managers in institutional systems creates pressures to keep caseloads up, even if the program is ineffective, and even if it causes harmful dependency. . . .

Rampant Fraud and Abuse

In exploring why government officials don't apply standards and don't demand performance of [welfare] recipients, it is useful to look at the problem of fraud. Comprehensive data on fraud and error in government programs are not readily available. Nevertheless, the partial data we do have indicate that it is a serious problem. The food stamp program has probably received more official attention than any other. Systems for detecting certain kinds of errors have been in place for more than twenty years, and they reveal a stubbornly high rate of error and abuse. In the mechanical process of giving out benefits, for example, there is a 10 percent error rate—a flaw that runs, as might be expected, in the direction of overpaying benefits. In 1995 these overpayments resulted in nearly $2 billion in excess payments. Another kind of abuse is trafficking—illegally selling food stamps for drugs, alcohol, cigarettes, and so on, instead of using them to purchase food. The General Accounting Office (GAO) estimates that 10 percent of benefits are trafficked.

The welfare program with the highest officially documented level of abuse is the earned income [tax] credit, the wage subsidy program that provides $20 billion in benefits. A careful audit by the IRS in 1988 found that 42 percent of recipients were overpaid and that erroneous benefit payments amounted to 34 percent of the total amount disbursed. A less comprehensive measure of the fraud in the program in 1994 found that $4.4 billion was falsely claimed and paid out.

Turning a Blind Eye to Fraud

All governmental attempts to determine the level of fraud in welfare programs have a double weakness: (1) officials are inclined to understate fraud because they are reluctant to let it be thought that their programs are seriously marred (the task commitment phenomenon), and (2) officials are unable to earn the confidence of welfare recipients to learn about all the misrepresentations they employ. For this reason, all official studies of welfare fraud greatly understate the true level of corruption. A valid study of welfare fraud would need to gain confidential information about the financial condition of the welfare recipients.

Perhaps the most searching study of this kind was conducted by Kathryn Edin in 1988 in a midwestern city. She gained the confidence of twenty-five women receiving Aid to Families with Dependent Children (AFDC) payments, who were introduced to her through friends, and found that all twenty-five had unreported income. Therefore, they all were defrauding the AFDC program. Most had unreported full- or part-time jobs; others were getting income from boyfriends and family members. This study suggests that the level of fraud in programs like AFDC and food stamps may be close to 100 percent, with virtually all recipients at least shading the truth about their financial circumstances and their ability to obtain outside income.

Welfare officials are often aware that high levels of fraud are occurring, but they seldom take strenuous steps to prevent it. Edin's research illustrates the point. She interviewed several dozen welfare case workers and pointed out that the reported budgets of many clients didn't add up, and that this had to mean they received unreported income. Though all the caseworkers agreed that this strongly indicated fraud, none of them wanted to act: "The case workers Edin interviewed all turned a blind eye to such indirect evidence of cheating because investigating a recipient's unreported income would have required extra work and would not have earned them any credit with their superiors."

Inherent Conflicts with Fraud Control

Welfare agencies and welfare workers are rewarded for higher caseloads and for dispensing more benefits. Since fraud control takes resources and only results in a reduced caseload, it is slighted. In a comprehensive book on fraud in the AFDC and Medicaid programs, John Gardiner and Theodore Lyman concluded that fraud control efforts are limited because "agencies' [fraud] control goals often conflict both operationally and politically with their service goals."

A good example of this pattern is the Social Security Administration's management of the federal disability system. Fraud in this system has attracted considerable media and congressional attention. In California, the complaints and tips about Supplemental Security Income (SSI) fraud became so numerous that the state Medi-Cal office conducted an investigation in 1993 using undercover agents posing as SSI claimants. Investigators uncovered systems of middlemen who coached clients in faking disabilities and medical practitioners who submitted phony reports. One clinic specialized in providing hundreds of diagnoses of "mildly mentally retarded" without even examining the claimants. That one clinic had fed 1,981 successful applicants into the SSI system, at a cost in benefits of $39 million.

Yet, the Social Security Administration (SSA) has refused to make a significant effort to control the fraud in its program. Indeed, it doesn't even want to hear about it. A House subcommittee found that workers in the disability field offices were dismayed by the stonewalling:

Many SSA field offices and State DDS [Disability Determination Service] offices informed the Subcommittee of their frustration with SSA headquarters and the HHS OIG

[Office of Inspector General of the Department of Health and Human Services]. Employees frequently recognized the pattern of fraud schemes by middlemen, only to have their referrals and complaints "fall on deaf ears." Eventually, some offices just quit making referrals.

The subcommittee noted that even after California investigators had exposed fraud schemes, the Social Security Administration dragged its feet doing anything about the documented abuses: "At the time of the hearing, SSA had not reopened any of the thousands of suspected SSI cases."

Confessions of a "Welfare Queen"

They called me a "welfare queen." I lived dependent upon the government for nearly seven years. I thrived on the welfare system. I defrauded it. I laughed at it. And I wasn't alone. . . .

My first benefit from welfare occurred in 1977, when, at age 21, I became pregnant for the first time—and I wasn't going to let a child interfere with my nightlife. I was working at a minimum-wage job without medical insurance. So to pay for an abortion, I simply bought a Medi-Cal sticker from a friend for $200.

Medi-Cal is California's government-run medical assistance program, and the participant was supposed to show her card at the clinic. However, some clinics would accept the sticker only, so that's what I provided. Without it, the procedure would have cost $400.

I first signed up for Aid to Families with Dependent Children (AFDC) in 1978. . . .

Six months later, I was pregnant again. This time I went to the county welfare office myself, because welfare would pay me immediately when I showed a doctor's note that said I was pregnant. My job paid $90 a week, but on AFDC welfare, I got $465 a month plus $80 in federal food stamps. What a deal! I quickly learned to pick up an extra $100 to $400 monthly by selling my extra Medi-Cal stickers. . . .

That biweekly check enabled me to continue as a prodigal. Without it, I wonder if I would have gotten pregnant four times and had four abortions. I wonder if I would have accepted help from my family instead of dismissing them as out of step. Instead, I got caught up in the welfare cycle, seduced by easy living that allowed me to do as I pleased. It would take me years to break free.

Star Parker, "Breaking the Bonds," *Family Voice*, March/April 2000.

Tolerance of Fraud Indicates Failure

Administrators say that fraud cannot be more energetically pursued because there are no funds for it. It's certainly true that antifraud efforts are expensive. To reopen, say, 1,981 suspected SSI claims—giving every case a complete hearing—would mean diverting many people from other administrative activities.

But what are those "other administrative activities"? Mainly, they are the work involved in getting people *on* the disability rolls. Nothing in the social security law requires the agency to give first priority to this function. The social security commissioner *could* recommend that the agency suspend taking new applications for as long as it takes to deal with the fraud backlog. But that, of course, would interfere with the doubling and redoubling of SSI rolls. . . .

The inability of government welfare programs to root out fraud in their programs is a warning sign. Before we can pronounce a government agency capable of expectant giving, capable of demanding an intricate quid pro quo from its beneficiaries, it first needs to prove that it has the will to prevent the massive cheating that has been going on for generations.

*"The [welfare] system makes us fraudulent.
. . . Because to get by, you have to do
things that [welfare caseworkers are] . . .
not going to allow."*

Insufficient Welfare Benefits Encourage Fraud

Karen Seccombe

In the following viewpoint, Karen Seccombe contends that welfare benefits are inadequate for raising a family. As a result, many recipients take on full- and part-time jobs, committing fraud by hiding this income from authorities. According to Seccombe, the welfare system itself is to blame for the prevalence of fraud. Women interviewed by Seccombe describe feeling trapped by a system that does not allow them to save enough money to permanently leave welfare. In the author's opinion, welfare fraud has become a strategy women use to meet the basic necessities. Karen Seccombe is a professor of sociology at Portland State University.

As you read, consider the following questions:

1. What percentage of the 214 welfare recipients interviewed by Kathyrn Edin and Laura Lein reported working jobs on the side during the past year, as cited by the author?
2. According to Seccombe, why are welfare recipients reluctant to report the income from temporary employment to their caseworkers?

W elfare recipients depend on multiple sources of assistance to supplement their welfare checks. They must piece together these important sources because their cash grant and food stamps do not provide enough money on which to live and raise their families. Those who live in subsidized housing can generally stretch their welfare assistance further than those women who pay full rent for their apartments, but even they usually have trouble making ends meet at the end of the month. Utility bills, clothing, diapers, school supplies, transportation, laundry costs, and routine household cleaning supplies, are some of the many items that deplete meager cash grants. Two hundred forty-one dollars a month, plus a couple of hundred dollars in food stamps, does not adequately cover even the low cost of living for an adult with one child. It also comes nowhere near lifting a family from poverty. Consequently, . . . women and their families turn to other relatives, if available, to help them out. They also turn to boyfriends, friends and neighbors, and to the fathers of their children. Yet, it's important to note that these sources of assistance are unpredictable, and are not available to all women. To round out their budget, women also turn to private and public charities and social service agencies for at least occasional assistance.

Supplementing the Welfare Check

These interviews revealed that even charities and social services agencies did not completely fill the gap between income and needs. Consequently, some women on welfare also work on the side, and often they did not report this income to the welfare office. Approximately one-quarter of the women interviewed informed me that they had recently worked at least sporadically to earn enough money to allow them to meet their monthly bills, buy food for their children, purchase the diapers or washing powder that food stamps cannot cover, or to buy their children a special treat in order to keep their spirits up. These findings echo those reported elsewhere. For example, estimates of unreported side jobs in the range of 20 percent were noted in the state of Wisconsin before Governor Tommy Thompson began his controversial welfare reform experiments. Kathryn Edin and Laura Lein (1997) report that 39 percent of the 214 women in their study reported to have worked jobs on the side during the past year (see Table 1).

Table 1: Survival Strategies of 165 Wage-Reliant Mothers

Variable	Amount of Income Generated Through Each Survival Strategy	Percent of Total Budget	Percent of Mothers Engaging in Each Survival Strategy
TOTAL EXPENSES	$1,243	100	N/A
Housing costs	341	24	N/A
Food costs	249	30	N/A
Other necessities	569	39	N/A
Nonessentials	84	7	N/A
TOTAL INCOME	1,226	100	N/A
Main job	777	63	100
Food stamps	57	5	28
SSI	3	0	2
EITC	25	2	28
Work-based strategies	88	7	39
Reported work	27	2	12
Unreported work	59	5	28
Underground work	2	0	1
Network-based strategies	253	21	82
Family and friends	65	5	47
Boyfriends	60	5	27
Absent fathers	127	10	42
Agency-based strategies	36	3	22

Kathryn Edin and Laura Lein, *Making Ends Meet: How Single Mothers Survive Welfare and Low-Wage Work*, 1997.

Jasmine, a 35-year-old African American woman who is divorced from her husband and has two children, bluntly explained the necessity of supplementing her welfare assistance so that she can maintain a reasonable standard of living for her family.

I may have some extras, like my telephone or cable bill, or something like that, but living these days and time, children need those things. We need a phone for emergencies and things, instead of having to walk to a neighbor or use a pay phone. To tell you the truth, I've been working little odd jobs on the side, like cleaning somebody's house or something like that to make ends meet. Also, there's a neighbor around the corner, and I've been taking him to the grocery store. He pays me $10 to take him up there to the grocery store, and I make money that way. Then, I also may go out in the fields, or something. You just have to do that to survive.

Sarah's story also reveals the necessity of side jobs in order to make it. Sarah is white, has three children, and is divorced from their father. The divorce was emotionally and financially complicated, and the difficulties are continuing as her husband attempts to gain custody of all their children. The children, some or all of them, divide time between Sarah and her ex-husband, who lives in a larger city approximately 70 miles away. Sarah currently works part-time at a fast food restaurant, and has informed her caseworker of her job. Her welfare benefits have been reduced accordingly, given her employment earnings. Sarah told me that it took her considerable time to find this position, despite having several years of experience working in the fast food industry, including experience as a manager. Before she found this position, and during a period when only one of her children lived with her, they relied on a variety of other "odd" jobs to make ends meet. These were not reported to her caseworker. She and her daughter could not survive on welfare alone: Her rent for her trailer, which is subsidized through a program at the community college, is $250 a month. Sarah's utilities average $100 a month, and she has a telephone and a small car payment. Therefore, her bills run approximately $500 a month, yet her cash grant for herself and her daughter was only $241. How did she make ends meet? First, she relied on a neighbor, Mrs. Janson, who let her stay at her place for a few months rent-free while Sarah saved her welfare checks. This allowed her to eventually move into her trailer.

If it wasn't for the school, and for my neighbor, me and my daughter would have been in the streets. But, between the school, Aid to Families with Dependent Children (AFDC), and Mrs. Janson letting me stay at her place, we could get this trailer. Otherwise we had no money and we would have fallen right through the cracks. But a lot of people don't have that extra help. And so that's what they do, they slide right into them cracks because there is nowhere else to go. They become homeless and draw inward because there is nowhere else to go.

Once in her trailer, Sarah faced the difficulty of trying to earn enough money on the side to continue to pay her recurring bills each month. She and her daughter, who wasn't yet in her teens, worked together in order to earn enough money to live. Her daughter's after-school hours were not spent in school sports, in clubs or organizations, or playing with friends. Rather, they were spent helping Sarah earn money to pay the utility bill.

> We cleaned houses; we raked people's yards. We did everything to get that extra money so they wouldn't turn off the utilities. We didn't have any money left over. If we had $5 or $6 at the end of the month, we went bowling. That was our one thing we did together. If we didn't have any money we went to [a specific park in town] because if you're on welfare you can get in for free. We did a lot of walking. For holidays, birthdays, or Christmas they got food.

Reporting Employment: Risky Business

The dilemma that many women face is whether to report these earnings to their caseworker. Legally, they are required to do so. In reality, some do, and some do not. I was told that caseworkers vary in the rigor in which they pursue such information, and vary in their likelihood of documenting temporary earnings. Some women told me that caseworkers were aggressively searching for evidence of fraud. Other women told me that some caseworkers will "let you get away with it." Leah told me how she handles trying to get additional money for Christmas, or other special occasions:

> Most of the time I try to do some temporary work. If I'm not employed, I try to get a lot of hours doing temporary work. Sometimes AFDC will let you get away with it. And sometimes, if you work during holidays, then come January and February, when you're not working anymore, they cut your AFDC and food stamps. So, if you do it, it depends on the caseworkers. They might just say, "Hey, since it was only a couple of months, we won't add it." And then again, some people add everything.

Some women are not willing to gamble with the generosity of a caseworker who may or may not break the rules to allow a woman to keep her earnings. Recipients know that if they earn something and report it now, it may take a month for the paperwork to go through the proper channels and reduce their grant. But, more importantly, if they are laid off, or if the temporary employment ceases, it may take another month for the paperwork to go through the system to allow their benefits to resume. During this time they will have no aid, and may experience considerable financial hardship. Women are well alerted to the fact that reporting employment, especially if it is unstable or temporary employment, can leave you and your family vulnerable. Therefore, many women choose to forgo telling their caseworker about extra income. I was frequently told about side jobs involving babysitting, hairstyling, doing nails, and providing transportation to others. A few other women worked in the formal sector, holding part or full-time jobs in the fast food industry, or a nursing home, and did not report the income to a caseworker. This is risky, as Dawn . . . found out. She was caught and convicted of welfare fraud. Yet Jo Lynn, a white woman with two children, believes working in the informal or formal sector or receiving benefits from friends or family that go unreported is commonplace. This is because of, she told me, the restrictive requirements and the low benefits afforded to recipients. She suggested that they simply cannot live on what they are given, and therefore must find a way to augment it.

> The system makes us fraudulent. It makes us fraudulent. I can tell you right now it makes everyone that is on the system fraudulent. They might as well tell you. They might as well tell you the truth. I'm fraudulent, and everybody else that I know is. Because to get by, you have to do things that they're not going to allow.

Double Dipping

Some women reported receiving extra income from boyfriends, or children's fathers, and most failed to report it to their caseworker. Legally, welfare recipients are required to report such "gifts," but most did not, especially if they saw the gift as a one-time or infrequent occurrence. They told me they could not afford to survive and raise their children without these gifts—they were one of the many ways to subsidize their meager cash grants. Some acknowledged, sheepishly, that they were breaking the rules, "I just hope they never catch up with us." Others rationalize it as a smart survival strategy. Coreen is a bright and ambitious 21-year-old African American mother of a toddler who "never thought I'd be on welfare." Her pregnancy was unplanned, and she lived with her mother, even sharing her mother's bed, until the crowded conditions became intolerable. She applied for welfare and moved into a small subsidized apartment, where she has resided for only a few months. Unknown to her caseworker, Coreen also works 30 hours a week at a fast food restaurant. Why is she cheating the welfare system? "I want to get ahead, and make something of myself," she tells me. She sees her "double dipping" as the only way to get off of welfare permanently. It will allow her the financial cushion she needs to continue college with the goal of being a teacher. It will allow her to move out of the housing projects, which she desperately detests. It will allow her and her boyfriend, who plan to marry soon, to save money so that they can have a fresh start. Welfare, she tells me, doesn't allow for this.

> As long as they give you money, they don't want you to better yourself, that is to say, have a job. This is how I truly feel. They cut your money as soon as you get a job. You can't have a bank account; you can't save money. I feel the system traps women. But I'm in school, and I'm not dropping out until I finish. . . . And I haven't told them I'm working yet because I feel like, it's not enough. With the money I make at [restaurant] that will only be enough for me to pay my bills and buy Pampers for my baby. That's not including clothes, socks, and stuff that she needs. They give you ten days; the last time I had a job they gave me ten days to report that I had a job. And then I lost my job, and I couldn't get a check for a whole month. That's not good. Me and my baby had to borrow, borrow, borrow. If they knew I was working they would take away the whole thing. And I have a boyfriend, and we are trying to move and get married and stuff. I mean, I feel good, because I know I have a future.

Coreen is clearly committing welfare fraud. She is taking money that she is not legally entitled to. Yet, despite the seriousness of her crime, many readers will not be altogether angry with her. . . . One of the major concerns with the welfare system is that it does not allow women the opportunity to amass the assets needed to exit welfare for good. Assets can cushion the difficulties that may seem to be minor irritants to the more affluent, but become unbearable on a minimum wage budget. Having assets can soften the blow when initial wages are held for a pay period; a car needs to be repaired; clothing or a uniform needs to be laundered or dry-cleaned regularly; or when a sick child cannot go to day care or school and a baby-sitter must be hired. Coreen, like others, knows that exiting welfare will be difficult. She feels that committing fraud by "double dipping" will at least give her a shot at it.

Each day, millions of welfare recipients piece together a broad array of strategies that allow them to meet the basic necessities of life. A fortunate few . . . have extended families who give help generously and graciously. Others are not so lucky. Living month to month, they resort to a variety of legal and illegal tactics to support their children. They live a tenuous existence between hope and despair.

"Child support enforcement program[s] will
. . . [move] more of America's poor families
toward self-sufficiency."

The Government Must Enforce Child Welfare Payments

Elaine Sorensen and Ariel Halpern

Fathers who shun financial responsibility for their children have been tagged "deadbeat dads" by welfare reformers. Reformers regard the behavior of these men as a major factor in child poverty and welfare costs. In the following viewpoint, Elaine Sorensen and Ariel Halpern maintain that aggressive collection of child support from these fathers is enabling more single mothers to move away from public assistance toward self-sufficiency. In addition to making child support enforcement available to all families, states have established programs to make paternity evasion more difficult for fathers, according to the authors. Sorensen is a labor economist and Halpern is a research associate at the Urban Institute, a nonpartisan domestic policy research organization.

As you read, consider the following questions:
1. As reported by the authors, what legislation did Congress enact in 1975 in response to father absence and growing welfare costs?
2. How did the 1996 welfare reform law continue the transformation of the child support enforcement system, according to Sorensen and Halpern?

The federal and state governments have devoted considerable resources to strengthening child support enforcement over the last two decades, but the proportion of single mothers who receive child support has remained largely unchanged. In 1997, 31 percent of single-mother families received child support, a figure that is only slightly higher than it was 20 years earlier (see figure 1). Although this trend appears impervious to government efforts to increase child support, in fact, considerable progress has been made for certain subgroups of single mothers. This progress is masked by a shift in the marital status composition of single mothers, away from divorced and separated mothers toward never-married mothers, with the latter having a much lower rate of child support receipt than the former.

Dramatic Gains in Receipt of Child Support

Improvements in child support receipt rates for some subgroups of single mothers result, in part, from strengthened child support enforcement policies enacted since the 1970s. The child support provisions under the most recent round of welfare reform will likely perpetuate the upward trend in child support receipt rates for many single mothers. To the extent that fathers have the ability to pay child support, continued investment in the child support enforcement program will mean that even more single mothers will be able to count on child support in the future.

Once we divide single mothers by their marital status, figure 1 shows that never-married mothers saw dramatic improvement in their child support receipt rate over the last two decades. Previously married mothers also experienced gains, though of a smaller magnitude. Never-married mothers experienced a fourfold increase in their child support receipt rate between 1976 and 1997, from 4 percent to 18 percent. Previously married mothers experienced a smaller increase, climbing from 36 percent to 42 percent.

The overall fraction of single mothers receiving child support remained largely unchanged during this period because the marital status composition of single-mother families changed dramatically. Figure 2 shows that, in 1976, 83 percent of single moms were divorced or separated (i.e., previously married); only 17 percent had never married. By 1997, the fraction of single moms who were divorced or separated had fallen to 54 percent. In other words, nearly half of single mothers are now in the never-married category.

Figure 1 shows that never-married mothers are much less likely to receive child support than are previously married mothers. Thus, despite significant progress in child support receipt by both never-married and previously married mothers, the dramatic change in the overall marital status composition of single mothers masks any gains in child support receipt.

Shift to More Aggressive Enforcement Strategies

Traditionally, the states' court systems have been responsible for establishing child support orders, determining their amount, and enforcing them. Since 1975, however, the federal and state governments have taken a more active role in child support enforcement, because of their fiscal responsibility for providing a safety net to poor children.

By the mid-1970s, it became clear to Congress that father absence was a major factor contributing to welfare costs and child poverty. Hence, Congress enacted Title IV-D of the Social Security Act in 1975, establishing an open-ended entitlement to child support enforcement services to all families receiving Aid to Families with Dependent Children (AFDC), as well as to any family requesting such services. This legislation created a federal/state partnership to enforce child support that remains largely unchanged to the present. Congress established the federal Office of Child Support Enforcement (OCSE) to oversee state child support enforcement programs but left the basic responsibility for administering the programs to the states. Every state was required to establish a child support enforcement (IV-D) agency, and the federal government agreed to reimburse 75 percent (later reduced to 66 percent) of the administrative costs of running these programs.

Since 1975, Congress has enacted major reforms of federal child support enforcement policies. Many of these reforms were first developed by state governments and found to be particularly effective enforcement tools. Once enforcement tools prove effective in specific states, the federal government will often require that all states adopt them. Figure 3 shows the year in which states adopted five such child support enforcement policies, all of which were subsequently mandated by the federal government. The sixth enforcement tool described in figure 3—the $50 pass-through—has had a different history. First mandated by the federal government in 1984 without prior state experimentation, it then became a state option in 1996. Today we see considerable state variation in implementation of the pass-through policy.

Implementing Enforcement Tools

The first challenge facing the federal/state partnership was to develop an efficient and effective system of collecting past-due child support from noncustodial parents who were behind in their child support payments. As a result, states began developing a series of enforcement tools to expedite these claims as well as to ensure their payment. One such enforcement tool—state tax intercept programs—was tried by many states, which established mechanisms to intercept state tax refunds from noncustodial parents who owe back child support. This reform, along with others,

Figure 1: Percent of Single Mothers Receiving Child Support, by Marital Status

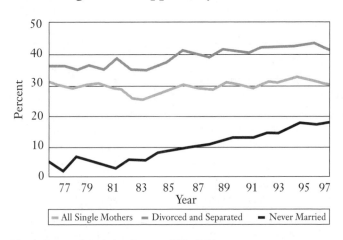

March Current Population Surveys 1977–1997.

was codified into federal law as part of the 1984 Child Support Enforcement Amendments.

Another enforcement tool—wage withholding—was originally applied only to delinquent obligors. Once noncustodial parents fell behind in their child support payments, states required judges to impose wage withholding. By the late 1980s, however, many states began to implement this mandate even before obligors became delinquent. Based on this experience, Congress enacted "immediate" wage withholding as part of the Family Support Act of 1988, which became effective in January 1994 for all new child support orders. Figure 3 indicates when states first adopted this policy.

States also began to address the lack of horizontal equity in the amounts of child support awards set by judges. Until the adoption of state child support guidelines, judges determined the amount of each award on a case-by-case basis, with no underlying formula to ensure consistency across families. States began to adopt child support guidelines in the 1970s, through either legislation, court rule, or administrative action. In 1984, the federal government required states to adopt advisory guidelines for judges' deliberations. In 1988, as part of the Family Support Act, Congress took the additional step of requiring states to make their child support guidelines binding on judges, or presumptive, unless a written finding was issued. States' adoption of presumptive guidelines is shown in figure 3.

Establishing Paternity and Employer Reporting

It was not until 1993 that Congress turned its attention to voluntary paternity establishment. Prior to that, although Congress had tried to make evasion of paternity more difficult for noncustodial fathers, it had not established a federal mandate that would allow noncustodial fathers to *voluntarily* acknowledge paternity. In response to successful in-hospital paternity programs in several states, Congress required all states to establish in-hospital paternity programs as part of the Omnibus Budget Reconciliation Act of 1993. As shown in figure 3, only five states had in-hospital paternity programs in 1993, the year Congress mandated them.

The latest federal effort to reform welfare, the Personal

Figure 2: Marital Status Composition of Single Mothers

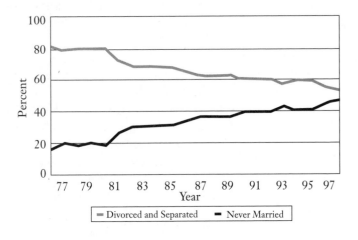

March Current Population Surveys 1977–1997.

Responsibility and Work Opportunity Reconciliation Act (PRWORA) of 1996, continued the transformation of the child support enforcement system by increasing its access to information and maintaining its effort to automate caseload processing. The legislation mandated that states require employers to report all new hires within 20 days to child support enforcement authorities. This new requirement is expected to reduce the delay in establishing immediate wage withholding.

PRWORA also eliminated the federal requirement that states pass through the first $50 of child support paid to welfare families. Following enactment of the child support enforcement program, any child support paid on behalf of a family receiving welfare (i.e., AFDC, replaced by Temporary Assistance for Needy Families [TANF]) was retained by the government to compensate it for the cost of providing aid to the family. After 1984, however, the federal government required states to pass through to the family the first $50 of child support received each month and disregard that amount in the determination of welfare benefits. This policy was meant to give the family on assistance an incentive to cooperate with the child support enforcement program. Under PRWORA, states are no longer required to pass through the first $50 of child support to welfare families. Figure 3 shows that 32 states have ceased providing a $50 pass-through.

Expanded Focus Beyond AFDC Mothers

Another policy shift over the last two decades has been to broaden the reach of the child support enforcement program beyond the AFDC population. Fiscal year (FY) 1997 is the first year in which there were more non-AFDC cases (52 percent) than AFDC cases in the IV-D program. In contrast, 20 years earlier, only 15 percent of the IV-D caseload con-

Figure 3: Trends in Child Support Policies

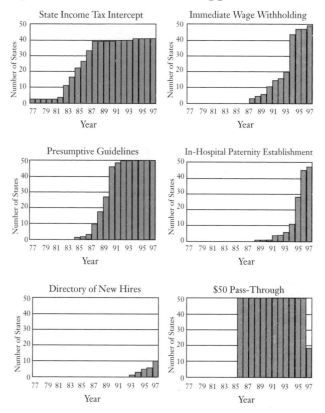

Authors' review of state statutes, supplemented when necessary by information from legal and policy staff at state child support enforcement offices.

sisted of non-AFDC cases. Since 1975, AFDC (and now TANF) recipients have had to assign their rights to child support to the government and cooperate with the IV-D program as a condition of receiving aid. Thus, all welfare families eligible for child support services are IV-D clients. Non-AFDC families, on the other hand, are eligible for services only if they request them. During the initial years of the IV-D program, essentially the entire focus of services was toward AFDC families. Federal matching funds were not available on a permanent basis to serve non-AFDC families until 1980. Incentive funding, which was available for AFDC collections, was not extended to non-AFDC collections until 1984. As Congress boosted the investment of federal dollars to serve non-AFDC families, states increased their efforts to serve this population.

As the child support enforcement program has grown in size and responsibilities, its expenditures have also grown. In FY 1997, the federal and state governments spent $3.4 billion on the child support enforcement program, whereas in FY 1976, they spent only $390 million (expressed in 1997 dollars). Caseloads have also grown during this period, increasing from 4.2 million in FY 1978 (the first year caseload data were reported) to 18.7 million in FY 1997. Thus, real expenditures per case have doubled during this period, from $93 per case in FY 1978 to $182 per case in FY 1997.

Tough Enforcement Gets Results

We estimate that 56 percent of the rise in child support receipt rates for never-married mothers and 33 percent of the rise in child support receipt rates for previously married mothers can be attributed to the six enforcement tools described in this analysis, as well as to the overall expansion of the child support enforcement program. . . . In other words, if these policies had not been enacted, we estimate that the never-married mothers' child support receipt rate would have increased by 6 rather than 14 percentage points and that the previously married mothers' child support receipt rate would have increased by only 4 instead of 6 percentage points.

With regard to specific child support enforcement policies, we find that the tax intercept program and presumptive child support guidelines significantly increased the likelihood of receiving child support for never-married and previously married mothers. In contrast, the voluntary in-hospital paternity establishment program significantly increased the child support receipt rate of never-married mothers but did not have a comparable result for previously married mothers. On the other hand, immediate wage withholding had a significantly positive impact on previously married mothers' child support receipt rate but not on that of never-married mothers.

More recent enforcement techniques, such as new-hire directories, which were included in the latest round of welfare reform, have not yet had an impact on single mothers' child support receipt. Most states had not adopted these provisions by 1997, when our data end. In contrast, numerous states eliminated the $50 pass-through in 1997, which actually reduced the amount of child support received by never-married mothers.

Looking Forward

As welfare reform has taken hold across the country, single mothers' reliance on private sources of income, including child support, has grown and will continue to do so. The child support enforcement program, with its expanded enforcement tools, has contributed to this trend, but shifts in the marital status composition of single mothers have masked resultant gains. Improving the efficiency and effectiveness of the child support enforcement program will result in greater numbers of single-mother families being able to count on child support, thereby moving more of America's poor families toward self-sufficiency. Without these continued improvements, child support will remain a dream for many poor children.

"Granting welfare to one party and asking a non-participating party to repay this [in the form of child support] is the ultimate in irresponsibility."

Noncustodial Fathers Should Not Be Required to Pay Child Support

John Smith

John Smith argues in the following viewpoint that child support enforcement unfairly punishes unwed or divorced fathers, referred to as "noncustodial parents," by subjecting them to invasion of privacy, loss of wages, and jail. Noncustodial parents should not have to repay the government for welfare services that a mother has received as a grant, often without the father's knowledge or consent, in the author's opinion. Smith is a research analyst with the Alliance for Non-Custodial Parents' Rights, an organization upholding the rights of fathers in child support and family law matters.

As you read, consider the following questions:

1. According to Smith, in what manner does the government's enforcement of child support laws invade the privacy of noncustodial parents?
2. What happens to the child support collected in welfare cases, as reported by the author?
3. In the author's opinion, what is an unintended side effect of child support orders for the families of noncustodial parents?

Excerpted from John Smith's written statement for the Hearing on Fatherhood to the House Committee on Ways and Means, Subcommittee on Human Resources, April 24, 1999.

C hild support hurts children. How could this be? After all, kids need to be clothed, housed and fed and that takes money. And child support collects this money for kids—at least in theory. Child support, with its excessive awards and draconian punishments, only serves to force noncustodial parents into exile, irreparably harming the children. Child support allows single-parent households to flourish.

Child Support Awards Are Excessive

Compare the average child support award against other government measures such as welfare, foster care, social security and the poverty level (see Table 1).

Even radical feminist and author Karen Winner confirms that child support is excessive when she writes, "There is accumulating evidence that men are challenging their wives for custody of the children precisely because it is cheaper to keep them than to pay child support." Custodial parents often complain about how low support orders are, but when suggested that they give up custody and *they* pay child support, the screams are deafening. If support orders were equitable, this wouldn't happen.

Congress has passed tougher and tougher legislation since child support's (Federal) inception in 1975—always hoping "this time it will work." It never has and it never will. The Constitution along with individual rights have taken a beating in the process. Today, child support is the only debt that one can be jailed for (debtor's prison), you can lose your driver's license (or any license) even though your "crime" had nothing to do with a car, invasion of privacy is rampant through government sponsored databases such as the Federal Parent Locator System (FPLS) and the National Directory of New Hires (NDNH). The Department of Health and Human Services' (HHS) FPLS tracks noncustodial parents' whereabouts and gives this information to custodial parents. However, if the custodial parent moves away with the children against court orders, as Geraldine Jensen, founder of the Association of Children for Enforcement of Support, Inc. (ACES) did, 1) they are not prosecuted for kidnapping (or violating a court order) and 2) HHS will not give the noncustodial parents information on their children's whereabouts. In other words, the FPLS is a one-way street. Administrative accountability is non-existent. Bureaucrats are free to ruin your life (e.g. false paternity assignments and incorrect reporting to credit bureaus), and they are legally absolved of any liability. It's open season on noncustodial parents.

Table 1: Child Support vs. Welfare Expenditures

Average Child Support Award	$733/mo	noncustodial parent's portion only
Foster Care	$358/mo	
Welfare (Michigan)	$87.80/mo*	$439/mo for a mother + 2 kids
Welfare (San Diego)	$128.57/mo*	$900/mo—mother + 4 kids (includes food stamps)
Average welfare benefit per recipient	$131.90/mo	Feb 1997 TANF
1997 Department of Health and Human Services (HHS) Adult Poverty Guidelines	$657.50/mo	$8,163 (1 adult under 65)
1997 HHS Child Poverty Guidelines	$221/mo	$10,815 (1 adult under 65 with 1 child under 18)
Social Security Adult Disability Income	$470/mo	

*Converted into "child equivalents" based on adult to child poverty ratio of 3:1.

The 1999 session of Congress had more "get tough" legislation introduced by Henry Hyde and Lynn Woolsey in addition to Christopher Cox, less than a year after President Clinton signed the Deadbeat Parents Punishment Act of 1998 into law. Child support and penalties accrue during unemployment and incarceration (even if you are a POW). The state of Georgia is considering "work camps" for noncustodial parents. Slavery is making a comeback.

Aside from the fact that parents are forced into exile by

our child support laws, no study has ever shown child support to help children. And how could it, since no accountability is required of custodial parents. Custodial parents can spend this tax-free gift on anything they want: booze, drugs, new clothes, a new car, vacations—maybe even on the children. Nobody knows how much of the money ever reaches the child. University of California at Los Angeles Professor William S. Comanor estimates that only $1 in $5 of child support actually is spent on the child. Why not adopt the same documentation rules for custodial parents that the IRS requires for tax deductions? Ditto for penalties and fines.

Studies do show that states highest in child support and welfare payments rank lowest in child well-being. . . . Why? Money is a destabilizer or put differently, a single-parent household enabler. What was responsible for increasing child well-being? The intact family, something not terribly popular with society's "me, me, me" attitude. Divorces increase during economic boom times and decrease during tough times. Child support, like welfare, creates an individual economic boom (without requiring work, no less).

Child support not only encourages irresponsible behavior, but demands it. Consider the case of the responsible non-custodial parent who works a second job to make up for the severe economic loss child support payments have created. He's doing what we would consider to be the responsible thing to do: improving himself, supporting his current family. The work ethic. He will have higher expenses, pay more taxes and have less time for himself and his family. But when the custodial parent hears of his second job, she files a petition for upward modification of child support based on his new increased income. The judge will grant this increase, as it is law. Net effect: the more responsible you are, the more child support punishes you. Why not cut back on your hours; even work less than full time? Enjoy yourself. Plus, you could use this as a form of revenge. The custodial parent has had all of her expenses paid for by the taxpayer (prosecution, attorneys, court fees, admin services). The noncustodial parent is forced to hire an attorney, file court papers and miss work—all direct expenses that he must pay. If he fails to do this, he will lose on default judgment.

Welfare: Grant or Loan?

Welfare is treated as a grant. The mother applies for welfare and gets it. The father has no say in the matter. If it were a loan, there would be principal, interest, late payment penalties and a length of the loan. For the mother, it is a grant—there is no intention of it ever being repaid, *by her*. But for the father, welfare that the mother applied for and received—often without his knowledge or consent—has now become a loan, complete with interest, penalties, even jail. For low-income fathers, it may be a moot point, as many do not earn enough to repay it.

For non-welfare fathers, why would anyone repay a loan that they had no say in obtaining? Granting welfare to one party and asking a non-participating party to repay this is the ultimate in irresponsibility. If a mother must go on welfare, the father should be offered custody of the children. If he assumes custody, then the mother would work (consistent with welfare to work policy) and pay the father child support.

Remember, collecting child support in welfare cases produces no benefit to the mother or children. All money goes back to the government. Please do not use the excuse that child support will lift children out of poverty.

An underlying problem with child support is that awards 1) do not reflect the dynamic nature of the economy and 2) are not necessarily based on earnings. Child support is based on a percentage of income, but not a dynamic or current percentage. If the child support order is calculated during a high earning period (overtime or commissions), then the noncustodial parent is stuck with a high order. Likewise, if the parent becomes disabled or gets laid off, child support ignores these facts. Why not make the percentage a true percentage? If your support order is 20% and you get laid off, 20% of $0 = $0.

Secondly, child support orders are often based on imputed wages—what the judge *thinks* you could or should be earning. Why not simply use reality? Disallow imputed earnings and base support on actual earnings. Imputed earnings, taken to extremes, becomes legalized indentured servitude—slavery. Another assault on the Constitution. The California

Supreme Court has already greased the slipperiest of all the slippery slopes with its 1998 Moss decision. . . .

Fundamental Problem 1: The Greed Factor

Children in poverty are on (or eligible for) welfare. All child support collected in welfare cases goes back to the government, not to the family. If welfare hasn't lifted these children out of poverty, it is impossible for child support to do so. Furthermore, child support advocates conveniently ignore the fact that many families of noncustodial parents are driven into poverty by child support orders. If all the unemployed, single custodial mothers worked minimum wage jobs, an additional $70 billion in household income would be available to children.

Child support encourages greed. It boils down to the premise that 1) poverty is the cause of poor child well-being and 2) money solves this problem. Money has never solved any social problem. LBJ's war on poverty is a perfect example. After spending trillions of dollars, poverty is alive and well. Studies have also shown that children raised below the poverty level academically outperformed children living above the poverty level—the reason: they were living in an intact family. As mentioned above, money is a single-parent household enabler, a destabilizer.

Current laws encourage custodial parents to get as much money as possible from the noncustodial parent. The Bureau of Family Support Operations in Los Angeles runs a public access TV program that urges custodial parents to ask for increases "because things change." Nationally recognized child support advocate Leora Gershenzon of The National Center for Youth Law, commenting on the large increase in establishing paternity orders, said, "Besides receiving child support, the children will benefit from access to the father's medical history, rights of inheritance and eligibility for the father's health insurance." The American Civil Liberties Union states, ". . . it is essential to consider ways to obtain an award that is higher than the basic amount dictated by the guidelines."

Greed is also encouraged within child support enforcement administration, as their funding is based on child support collected (or amount to be collected). If the goal is to increase child well-being, why not base performance incentives of these organizations on child well-being instead of money collected? The fact that child support collections has become a big business is another clue to its greediness. Lockheed-Martin, the world's largest defense contractor, states that child support collection is "the company's fastest-growing line of business." In today's one-sided atmosphere of "anything goes," private collection companies have no qualms boasting about how they intrude on noncustodial parents' rights and why these parents shouldn't have any rights.

Fundamental Problem 2: The Revenge Factor

The concept of custody (or primary caretaker) is the perfect vehicle for revenge and is used everyday for just that. Why do we treat children like property? "She got the house, the car and the kids." We've all heard it. When children are treated like property (coldly and callously), they act coldly and callously and we get situations like Littleton, Colorado. We are reaping what we've sown. Our children are not suffering from too much parental involvement, they are suffering from a lack of it, as is all of society. When our children are not raised properly, everyone pays the price. Time is needed to instill values in children. When sole custody is awarded (sometimes under the name of joint custody), not only does the child lose contact with that parent, but the custodial parent is apt to suffer from what Dr. Richard Warshak calls "overload"—trying to be a full-time parent while holding down a full-time job. Depression, anger and hopelessness result.

While billions of dollars are spent annually to enforce child support, nothing is spent on enforcing visitation. Visitation violations are as common as clouds in the sky, yet they are not prosecuted. People like ACES' founder Geraldine Jensen know they can break the law with no repercussions. HHS proudly announced that they have made $10 million in grants available to study access (visitation). How does this $10 million nation-wide figure compare to support enforcement? Los Angeles County alone spends $120 million each year (and now wants to raise this 6 fold to $720 million). Adding insult to injury, a Children's Rights Council member in Toledo notes that many of these grants are going to battered women's shelters and other distinctly anti-male, anti-father and anti-family groups. Actions speak louder than words.

False allegations of abuse (spousal and/or child sexual) represent the largest social problem facing our nation. False abuse claims are frequently used during custody hearings. Because no trial is given and no evidence required, false abuse is the perfect vehicle to gain instant custody of your child. By the time your trial comes around, no judge will remove a child from the parent who issued the TRO (temporary restraining order). The party that lies, wins. What is needed is a strict physical evidence standard in all abuse cases. Period. Vigorous prosecution of people making false claims should follow. False abuse allegations should carry stiffer penalties than the abuse penalty itself, as the person is knowingly defrauding an innocent person.

Child Support as a Last Resort

When a couple has a child, they have made an 18-year commitment—regardless of their marital status. Children have the *right* to be raised by both biological parents and the parents have a *responsibility* to raise their children. As a society, we need to demand accountability for their actions. If you don't think you can stay with your partner for 18 years, you have no business having a child. "Move-aways" would be strictly prohibited unless otherwise agreed to in a written shared parenting plan.

Make shared parenting a rebuttable presumption in all divorce and child support cases, when parents cannot reach a voluntary agreement. Shared parenting is based on a written plan (unlike joint custody) and requires both parents to spend equal time (unless otherwise agreed to) raising their children. Shared parenting focuses on physical time spent with children and most closely emulates the child's environment prior to divorce. Since each parent is spending equal time and resources raising their children, the need for child support collections evaporates. Child support would only be collected in cases where one parent refuses to either 1) spend half their time raising their children or 2) follow an agreed upon parenting plan.

With child support eliminated, the greed factor is eliminated. Parents know they cannot continually go back to court and ask for more money (plus, free resources would not be available to them). With the concept of custody dissolved, the revenge factor disappears—there is nothing to fight over. If false allegations of abuse (that cannot be backed up with physical evidence) are made, watch out—you're headed for jail. If you move away with your kids (of course, they are not *your* kids), you will be prosecuted for kidnapping, unless agreed to in your parenting plan. With the greed and revenge factors eliminated, parents can now concentrate on what they should have been doing all along: getting on with their life.

The most likely argument against this is that restricting "move-aways" violates a person's freedom of movement. Once a couple has children, their freedoms temporarily are overridden by the child's need to have both parents and the parent's responsibilities. If a parent wants to wander, then don't have kids. It's time to enforce responsible behavior and hold people accountable for their actions.

Time to Abandon Failed Policy

Continuous introduction of child support legislation and increasingly draconian punishments reflect the frustration of 24 years worth of failed policy. With each new failure, the same "get tough" mantra is repeated instead of looking for new, fair and permanent solutions. Personal responsibility is defined as zipping off a check once a month and only applies to noncustodial parents.

Thinking that low-income fathers can be "fixed" has two major flaws. First, if the low-income group becomes middle-income, then child support problems will simply shift into this category and not be solved. Secondly, if low-income fathers are put to work simply so the government can take the money they earned and pay it to the mother—why work? In many cases, child support is 50% of a person's gross pay. This explains why many quit after their employer informs them of a wage garnishment. Getting a new minimum wage job becomes an instant doubling of their pay.

While societal change is an unclear and long process, our

laws can, and must, be changed now—switching their sole focus from money to increasing parental involvement. This means maximizing the involvement of both parents. Shared parenting is the mechanism to do this. The greed and revenge factors would be eliminated from family law. A strong message of the work ethic, personal responsibility and accountability is what these new laws must promote and reinforce. Kids need parents, not money.

| *"The new temporary-assistance [welfare] program is . . . out of sync with the needs of refugees."*

Refugees Deserve Welfare Assistance from the Government

Sara Paretsky

Thousands of refugee families arrive in the United States each year. Many of these families are channeled into state welfare programs where they must comply with work or work-training requirements and are subject to time limits on assistance. Sara Paretsky maintains in the following viewpoint that it is unfair to expect refugees, who are unfamiliar with English and recovering from stressful events, to adhere to the same timetables as people born and raised in the United States. The author contends that the federal government should provide refugees with a year of cash and medical assistance while they adjust to their new country, freeing states to concentrate on needy families already living in America. Paretsky is the granddaughter of a Lithuanian refugee and the author of the novel *Ghost Country*.

As you read, consider the following questions:

1. How much money do state agencies receive from the federal government to cover the first thirty days of a refugee's basic needs, according to the author?
2. In the author's opinion, what hardships must refugees endure to comply with the same welfare rules as native-born Americans?

When Ethel Krupnik was 12, soldiers broke into her home near Vilna, Lithuania, in the middle of the night and shot her father dead as she and the rest of her family cowered in the kitchen. Her mother, fearing that Ethel would be killed in turn—her education, including the four languages she spoke, made her seem threatening to neighbors—sent the girl to a cousin in New York.

It was 1911, the year of a pogrom in Eastern Europe that produced a lot of refugees bound for America. The United States didn't have a complicated refugee policy then; if you could make it to an entry port and pass the health inspection, you were here. Neither the Federal nor the state governments offered any assistance to immigrants or refugees, who sank or swam as best they could. When Ethel's cousin refused to support his penniless relation and left her on her own on the streets of the great city, she survived by hemming shirt-waists in a sweatshop.

Nowadays it would be much harder for Ethel to get into this country, but if she were one of the 20,000 Kosovars the United States is accepting from among the 779,000 driven out of their homes by Serb terrorism, a state agency would get around $500 in Federal money to cover her basic needs in the first 30 days. After 30 days she would be turned over to the public-assistance program in the state where the Federal Government sent her. There she would be covered by the welfare-reform law known as Temporary Assistance to Needy Families or by Refugee Cash Assistance, the program for adults without children.

Problematic Standards and Timetables

The majority of refugees now arriving in this country are families with dependent children. Unfortunately, the temporary-assistance program lumps together all needy families, immigrant or not. Refugees who have just survived the most shocking scenes of violence and violation and who may speak no English, let alone understand how to navigate our culture, run under the same rules and the same timetable as people born and brought up in the United States.

Briefly, when we reformed the country's welfare laws in 1996, we eliminated Aid to Families with Dependent Chil-

Tough Work Requirements for Refugees

As federal work participation requirements increase and welfare caseloads decrease, the percentage of recipients that must be in work to meet federal requirements becomes even more critical and more difficult to attain, as those who remain on welfare typically have multiple barriers to employment. States with immigrant and refugee populations must consider the long-term needs of these families, because their ability to attain self-sufficiency through work will directly affect a state's ability to meet federal work participation rates. To qualify for the full amount of their Temporary Assistance for Needy Families (TANF) block grant under federal welfare reform, states must demonstrate that 25 percent of all welfare recipients worked 20 hours per week in fiscal year (FY) 1997. These requirements increase incrementally until 50 percent of all welfare recipients are required to be in work in 2002, and to be working 30 hours per week by the year 2000. In addition to the participation rates for all families that receive TANF, the Personal Responsibility and Work Opportunity Reconciliation Act (PRWORA) established significant work requirements for states' two-parent TANF caseloads. Rigid two-parent rates required that, in FY 1997, 75 percent of all two-parent families worked 35 hours per week, increasing to 90 percent in 1999. States with refugee populations will be particularly affected by two-parent work rates, because many refugee families that receive assistance are part of a state's two-parent caseload. For example, in Cook County, Illinois, 60 percent of the two-parent families that receive assistance are refugees.

Anne Morse et al., *America's Newcomers: Mending the Safety Net for Immigrants.* Washington, DC: National Conference of State Legislatures, April 1998.

---

dren, long a fixture of the welfare system, and went to a work-based model—meaning we were no longer stressing the needs of dependent children but pushing to get adults into the work force. Congress hoped to break what it saw as the cycle of many generations living on welfare without the skills or incentives to join the work force. However good or bad the new temporary-assistance program is, it is out of sync with the needs of refugees.

Under the program, the Federal Government gives states block grants to use in supporting needy residents. The states can devise whatever programs they want, but the Federal

Government sets standards that the states have to meet in order to get the maximum amount of money. One requirement is that 90 percent of adults in temporary-assistance households be in some kind of work or work-training program. A single parent has to do 30 hours a week; in a two-parent home, the total is 35 hours.

Adults with young children are covered for a maximum of five years, but the state can choose a shorter maximum. And Federal incentives encourage states to keep shrinking their caseloads.

Expecting Too Much from Refugees

Applying the same rules to refugees and to people who were born here causes several hardships. It is difficult for someone just learning the language, and often recovering from severe stress, to get 35 hours of authorized work activity a week. And it is punitive to both refugees and the states to count new refugees as part of state welfare caseloads.

The State Department allocates refugees among the states. The numbers remain fairly constant: New York gets about 10,700 new refugees every year, Illinois about 4,000 and New Jersey around 1,400. No matter how many people find jobs, the number of refugees on temporary assistance remains constant because each year newly arriving refugees are added to state welfare rolls.

It is a mistake to penalize states for providing services to a group of needy people whose presence on the temporary-assistance rolls is inappropriate in the first place. And if the Federal Government puts too much pressure on the states to cut caseloads, we will be in the position of bringing Kosovars, or Rwandans, or other desperate and terrified people, into the country and treating them the way Ethel's cousin treated her: throwing them onto the street with no concern for how they'll survive.

Smoothing the Transition

We have a great opportunity now, in the wake of the Kosovo nightmare, to amend Federal policy so that refugees are not lumped together with those born and brought up here. The Federal Government should provide specialized cash and medical assistance to refugees during their first year in this country while they learn English, recover from the trauma of the violence they have witnessed and learn how to navigate a sophisticated job culture. That way the states could concentrate on the needy families that already live here.

Refugees are survivors. They want sanctuary and a chance to achieve and contribute, but it takes a reasonable period after arrival for them to find their way in an alien land.

A year's eligibility for specialized Federal cash and medical assistance would come back many times over in the productivity that refugee families ultimately generate. Ask Ethel's family: her seven surviving grandchildren paid around $600,000 in Federal income taxes in 1998. I'm one of those seven. I'd like America to open its doors as widely as possible to the victims of persecution. And I'd like my Federal tax dollars to help other Ethels make an easier transition to their new homeland.

"The usual incentives and disincentives [to refugee assimilation] do not function when cash, food, housing, and medical care are available upon arrival."

Refugees Should Be Discouraged from Accepting Welfare

Don Barnett

In the following viewpoint, freelance writer Don Barnett argues that the government should not offer refugees welfare benefits upon arrival. According to Barnett, publicly funded agencies involved with refugee resettlement encourage refugees to take advantage of federal welfare programs but provide little in the way of actual resettlement support. As a result, refugees lack the incentive to quickly integrate themselves into American culture by learning English and finding work, and a large number have become dependent on welfare programs.

As you read, consider the following questions:

1. According to Barnett, what sorts of programs were state welfare administrators encouraging refugees to tap into at the conference held by the Office of Refugee Resettlement?
2. In a 1996 federal study, what percentage of refugee households were receiving cash assistance?
3. In Barnett's opinion, what has replaced persecution as the engine of refugee migration to the United States?

Excerpted from "Show Me the Money: How Government Funding Has Corrupted Refugee Resettlement," by Don Barnett, *Center for Immigration Studies Backgrounder*, April 1999. Copyright © 1999 by the Center for Immigration Studies. Reprinted with permission.

O ver Veterans' Day in 1998, 1,200 private charity staffers, lawyers, and lobbyists as well as federal, state, and local government officials converged on the Mayflower Hotel in Washington, D.C., for the largest annual conference ever held by the Office of Refugee Resettlement (ORR), a division of the Department of Health and Human Services (HHS).

All "About the Money"

In contrast to the media horde which was to descend on the Mayflower when [former presidential intern] Monica Lewinsky arrived two months later, not one reporter was there to cover the event. This lack of media curiosity is puzzling given the heightened visibility of refugees in the world today and the impact of the refugee resettlement program on immigration to the United States.

The conference centered on 60 workshops punctuated by speeches from a cabinet member, lobbyists, and federal agency directors, as well as a message from the Dalai Lama. Called "Becoming American: From Refugee to Citizen," the conference would more aptly have been named "Becoming American: Getting and Keeping Public Benefits."

Most of the workshops, to greater or lesser degrees, were "about the money" as one presenter put it; for three days the opulent hotel seemed to be carpeted with money from federal grants. (ORR alone has about 200 grants up for grabs according to its latest report to Congress.) Federal refugee aid runs from the general—a grant to "expose newcomers to American Social Services"—to the specific—a grant for "rehabilitative counseling for refugee men who are batterers." Beside the opportunity to learn how to qualify for refugee-specific grant money, there were workshops on how to tap into much broader federal initiatives. Health care programs, bilingual education, housing programs, federal money for crime fighting, and Justice Department civil rights attorneys are just some of the resources available to agencies resettling refugees in the United States.

In one session, a state welfare administrator explained how to minimize the impact of the new work requirements for refugee welfare recipients, while a county official explained how to avoid them altogether. In another workshop, conferees learned how to turn a donated mattress into federal money by giving the mattress a dollar value and then claiming a matching grant from the government under the Federal Match Grant program. Under this misnamed program, every dollar's worth of donated goods or volunteer time is matched by $1.40 from the federal government.

Exploiting Health Care Services

A financial analyst at HHS saw opportunities in the Children's Health Insurance Policy (CHIP), the five-year, $25 billion expansion of Medicaid that targets children of mothers leaving welfare for work. According to this expert, CHIP money can be used for refugee TB screening—even though all immigrants and refugees should be TB-free—since according to ORR "overseas screening for certain diseases, especially TB, has been found to be unreliable." In fact, The Centers for Disease Control (CDC) reports that the foreign born currently account for 39 percent of all TB cases in the United States and, if current trends continue, will account for over half of all cases within 10 years. The data for Hepatitis B are similar: the foreign born account for 40 to 60 percent of all cases. In addition, we are told that CHIP can be used to educate refugees about the dangers of female genital mutilation (FGM), though there was disagreement as to how to do this in a "culturally appropriate" manner. CDC recently estimated that more than 150,000 women and girls in the United States may be at risk for or have already been subjected to the operation. Conferees confirmed a back alley practice in the operation, which leads one to wonder just how safe America is for women fleeing FGM in their home countries.

"Linguistically and culturally appropriate" social services were a popular topic at the conference. The California state refugee office publishes its brochure on domestic violence in 11 languages, but according to the state refugee health coordinator even this is "linguistically and culturally" inadequate for the needs of newer refugee arrivals. In spite of the fact that even state refugee agencies seem unable to stay relevant, the conference panel on refugee health care suggested using the local Office of Civil Rights to sue hospitals for discrimination if they cannot provide services (including mental health) in the language of the person demanding those services. Meanwhile, HHS Director Donna Shalala urged participants to use refugee health problems as a cudgel in the fight for universal health care. (A commonly heard argument is that only free health care can guard against the threat of an epidemic.) Yet conference speakers discussed cases where free TB treatment was refused by refugees in the United States for "cultural" reasons and agreed that free U.S. government TB screening and treatment available to refugees before departure to the United States has clearly failed.

At the INS workshop, conference participants learned (from an INS employee no less) that "private" service providers, unlike government agencies, need not verify the legal status of the beneficiaries of their services, even though they are basically dispensing government benefits.

Charities on the Dole

The Voluntary Agencies (Volags) involved in refugee resettlement insist on calling themselves private charities. At one time this was true. Prior to the mid-1970s, refugee sponsorship was mostly the work of private charities, but with the Refugee Act of 1980 public funds have dominated all aspects of refugee resettlement. Even in the 1980s and early 1990s the Private Sector Initiative program allowed sponsoring organizations to bring over refugees if they were willing to cover costs of resettlement and support after arrival, but Volags, preferring to lobby for increased government support of refugees, shunned the private program and it was discontinued in 1995 for lack of use. Public money always drives out private money. Put another way by a state refugee official at the conference who asked not to be named: "Volags only do what the state pays for." The two largest Volags—U.S. Catholic Charities and the Hebrew Immigrant Aid Society—together received about $75 million in State Department and ORR funds for their U.S. operations alone in 1996, the last year for which data is available, and a Volag affiliate boasts in a publication that money "pours" in from local and state governments as well.

Naturally this money is meant to be used to help refugees. But the Volags have astonishingly meager responsibilities for actual resettlement and support of the refugees they sponsor. The Volags do not even guarantee the federal loans made to the refugees for airfare to the United States. (Less than half of the loans made for this purpose since the 70s have been paid back, leaving an unpaid bill of $415 million.) Judging from this conference, their main function is to get refugees on federal welfare programs as soon as possible.

Refugees Admitted to the United States, 1990–1998

	East Asia	Near East/ S. Asia	USSR & E. Europe	Africa	Latin America	Total
1990	51,611	4,991	56,912	3,494	2,309	**119,317**
1991	53,486	5,539	45,516	4,424	2,237	**111,022**
1992	51,848	6,844	64,184	5,491	2,924	**131,291**
1993	49,858	7,000	51,278	6,969	4,126	**119,231**
1994	43,581	5,861	50,947	5,856	6,437	**112,682**
1995	36,926	4,464	45,703	4,779	7,618	**99,490**
1996	19,235	3,788	41,617	7,512	3,541	**75,693**
1997	8,590	3,990	48,450	6,069	2,986	**70,085**
1998	10,848	3,197	54,260	6,662	1,587	**76,554**

Refugee Reports, vol. 19, no. 12.

Every refugee resettled in the United States is assigned to one of 10 Volags, adding to that agency's headcount and therefore federal cash allotment. In many cases the Volag's responsibility for the refugees it sponsors is virtually nil, though in fairness it must be noted that a Volag often has little choice over individuals assigned to it. Refugee recruitment largely takes place independently of both the Volags and the U.S. government.

Cheryl Smith, director of Sacramento County Social Services, describes a Pentecostal church that expands its membership through missionary activity in Ukraine. The church members are initially placed in cities around the United States by the State Department and the Volags. But with their true destination the community that first contacted them, the religious refugees quickly undertake a second migration to Sacramento, leaving the Volag "sponsor" a mere observer rather than a participant with a stake in the process.

In the case of the Pentecostal church, the pastor, church leadership, and most of the members are dependent on welfare, as is the whole informal refugee sponsorship network. In this case it was Pentacostals, but according to the FBI about 2,000 Russian organized crime operatives had been sponsored into the country on the refugee program by 1996. (Another 2,000 arrived illegally.)

Bullish on Citizenship

Citizenship was the theme of this year's conference. Promoted in clinics paid for with tax dollars, it was touted as a way to maintain access to federal benefit programs. Refugees are exempt for seven years from the bar on welfare usage that applies to other new immigrants. After seven years, they must become citizens in order to maintain access to some federal benefits. State and local agencies prefer dependence on federal programs over dependence on local programs. Accordingly, both private and governmental agencies use tax dollars in citizenship drives for everything from coaching to transportation and INS processing fees. Mass mailings inform noncitizen welfare recipients of the need to naturalize in order to avoid losing their entitlements. State programs, such as the Massachusetts Citizenship Assistance Program, target those "who are receiving state-funded benefits that could be replaced with federal benefits were they to become citizens." The state has set up a 24-hour hotline to reach this segment of the population with its message about the advantages of citizenship.

Recognizing the new value of citizenship, the Volags have also leveraged their tax dollars to promote citizenship—U.S. Catholic Charities uses Americorp staff for the task. One agency offers a brochure on how to qualify as disabled for purposes of taking the simplified citizenship exam in one's own language. In a reversal of traditional notions of citizenship, the more mentally incompetent the applicant is, the easier it is to gain citizenship.

Welfare Matters

Legally, refugees and asylees are eligible for all welfare on the same basis as U.S. citizens within 30 days of arrival.

(Asylees are those who are already in the United States when they seek the right of permanent U.S. residency based on a claim that they would be persecuted if returned home.) A 1996 federal study of refugees arriving in the previous five years found that 46 percent of refugee households were receiving cash assistance. Approximately 48 percent of the households received food stamps. About 12 percent of refugee households were in public housing with possibly another 12 percent on waiting lists for public housing or Section 8 housing. These figures are quite startling in view of the fact that 75 to 80 percent of refugee arrivals are joining family members who settled in previous waves.

Total welfare usage by refugees cannot be determined. Three years after welfare reform, however, there are about 203,000 *noncitizen* refugees and their children receiving federal cash assistance through Temporary Assistance for Needy Families (TANF) and/or Supplemental Security Income (SSI) in California alone. No one knows the number of citizen refugees receiving federal cash assistance in California because it is not tracked, but it could be equal to or greater than the number of dependent noncitizen refugees. Further, based on studies that track welfare usage for five years after arrival, refugees typically use local general assistance cash at even higher levels than either TANF or SSI. California is home to about a quarter of the nation's refugees. Generalizing to the rest of the nation is risky, but the California data suggest that substantial long-term welfare dependence is the norm for many refugees. Without welfare there would be no refugee resettlement program as we know it.

A Break with American Tradition

Dismantling private sponsorship has changed the basic assumptions that guaranteed the integrity of earlier refugee resettlement. First, it obviated the need to integrate refugees as soon as possible into the language, economy, and host community. The usual incentives and disincentives do not function when cash, food, housing, and medical care are available upon arrival. Perhaps most importantly it has induced many to immigrate who otherwise would never have entertained the notion, furthering the development of enclaves of those who cannot or will not assimilate. It also raised politics and management of public opinion to new levels—"controlling the agenda" was one of the themes at this year's conference. At a strategy session of refugee advocates and publicists at another conference I attended, an attorney leading the session explained that winning public opinion and congressional support depended on controlling the terms of the debate. Fencing discussion in with a framework of "refugees" who are always "fleeing for their lives" shuts down the opposition every time. When I pointed out that the very use of the term "refugee" for most of those entering on the refugee program was an example of controlling and defining the terms of the debate he readily agreed, and went on to say that many staffers at his own resettlement agency refuse to use the term "refugee" and pointedly refer to the new arrivals as "those people."

There needn't be any worry over media treatment of the subject. Such reporting as there is consists mainly of stories about mistreatment of individuals at the hands of the immigration system. The overwhelming impression from media accounts, for instance, is that asylee flows have been choked down to a trickle by draconian new laws and that innocent applicants are being thrown in jail or deported to life threatening situations at home. *The New York Times*, analyzing a six-month period of immigration data, reported in June of 1998 that "from August of last year through the end of January . . . 1,300 new arrivals expressed a fear to return home. Of those, 1,066 were sent to detention; the rest were deported." Nowhere does the article state that this data relates only to the tiniest source of asylum applications—those who show up at airports without valid documents and file for asylum. Most asylum seekers apply after their temporary visas expire or after successfully entering the country on bogus documents. In fact, about 59,000 new applications for asylum were made in 1997. This represents about 88,500 individuals, far exceeding the expected flow implied in the law and not including an additional 30,000 whose applications from previous years were reconsidered under appeal. Annual asylum applicants exceed the number implied in the *Time*s article by a factor of 34. Less than 5 percent of asylum applicants are ever held in detention and those that are spend an average of less than three months in detention. In addition, they have the right to withdraw their applications and return home at any time. . . .

Increasing the Refugee Burden

Both refugee and asylee numbers have already vastly outstripped all projections made when the 1980 Refugee Act was signed. Public sponsorship allowed numbers to go much higher than would have been possible with private sponsorship and removed all effective controls over the process except for the political. Maybe that's why in most cases group preferences and family-chain migration have replaced persecution as the engine of refugee migration to the United States.

In FY 1998, about 77,000 refugees were resettled permanently to the United States, not including 20,000 Cubans who arrived with most of the same rights and entitlements as refugees. Additionally, though final numbers are unavailable, new applications for asylum were filed for at least 80,000 individuals in 1998. (These figures do not include recent "one-time" amnesties for 200,000 Central Americans, Cubans and Haitians, temporary protected status for certain nationals who have overstayed their visas, or smaller humanitarian immigration programs.) . . .

The main Volags are calling for a refugee admission ceiling of 111,000, an increase of 44 percent over current numbers, arguing in part that larger numbers are necessary to justify overhead and staff in the private charities.

Many of the jobs they are trying to protect are held by the new arrivals themselves. Refugee resettlement has grown into a substantial public/private enterprise directly employing thousands and equaling if not exceeding the U.S. foreign aid budget in its demands for public money when the cost of long-term public assistance is counted. Indeed the private and the public are hardly distinguishable. Julia Taft, formerly the director of the consortium of private charities requesting an increase in the annual refugee quota, is now the director of the State Department bureau that makes the U.S. government's recommendation for that quota. According to federal and state sources, the second in charge at ORR recently left his government job for a position as the Executive Vice President at the largest resettlement agency, at an annual salary in excess of $200,000 per year.

There is nothing new about a federal program that has gone off the tracks. The circular arrangements that make the refugee program work characterize many of our public institutions, but few share the refugee program's potential to so radically change America. ("We are re-inventing America!" proclaimed a speaker.)

From the *Mayflower* to the Mayflower Hotel

There was much to celebrate at this year's ORR conference and the mood was positively exultant. The refugee resettlement program, protected by an impenetrable shell of myth and supported by a diverse set of interlocking interests and coalitions, could count on continued congressional support. Lobbying efforts to overturn some of the welfare reforms that affected immigrants had paid off and there was every reason to believe more concessions were on the way.

The reality of life in a refugee camp hardly intruded on the sumptuous meals and cocktail hours at the Mayflower Hotel. There was a Veteran's Day moment of silence, but the only veterans mentioned were the conferees themselves—"veteran refugee workers" and Red Army vets living in Brooklyn who won a great victory when their welfare/Medicaid was restored. It was a fitting symbol for much of the refugee program today.

Periodical Bibliography

The following articles have been selected to supplement the diverse views presented in this chapter.

David Barstow   "ATM Cards Fail to Live Up to Promises to Poor," *New York Times*, August 16, 1999.

David Byrd   "Making Dad Matter," *National Journal*, April 15, 2000.

Christopher D. Cook   "To Combat Welfare Fraud, States Reach for Debit Cards," *Christian Science Monitor*, May 25, 1999.

Jason DeParle   "Welfare Overhaul Initiatives Focus on Fathers," *New York Times*, September 3, 1998.

Terry Everett   "Rooting Out Welfare and Food Stamp Fraud," U.S. House of Representatives, August 10, 1998. www.house.gov.

Margaret A. Jacobs   "Prodding Unwed Dads to Admit Paternity," *Wall Street Journal*, October 16, 1997.

Stuart A. Miller   "The Myth of Deadbeat Dads," National Organization for Men, January 15, 2000. www.tnom.com.

Jeff Minerd   "A Kinder, Gentler Look at 'Deadbeat Dads,'" *Futurist*, May 1999.

Evelyn Nieves   "Can a Couple Find Luxury on Welfare?" *New York Times*, March 27, 1997.

Sean Paige   "Fighting Fraud from Abroad," *Insight on the News*, June 29, 1998.

Christopher Reed   "Secrets and Wives," *Bulletin with Newsweek*, April 20, 1999.

Joe Sexton   "In a Pocket of Brooklyn Sewn by Welfare, an Unraveling," *New York Times*, March 10, 1997.

Joe Sexton   "In Brooklyn Neighborhood, Welfare Fraud Is Nothing New," *New York Times*, March 19, 1997.

Barbara Vobejda and Judith Havemann   "Welfare Clients Already Work, Off the Books; Experts Say Side Income Could Hamper Reforms," *Washington Post*, November 3, 1997.

CHAPTER 3

Can Private Efforts Replace the Welfare System?

Chapter Preface

In the late nineteenth and early twentieth centuries, most Americans toiled at low-wage factory or agricultural work without health insurance, pensions, or a welfare safety net to rely on during periods of unemployment. The loss of a job or the death of a husband often left families destitute. Since the government took little responsibility for the poor, private charities and limited state-run poverty programs were the only sources of support in times of need.

Confronted with widespread poverty and unemployment during the Great Depression of the 1930s, the federal government instituted the large-scale public assistance programs of the New Deal, greatly reducing the role of private charities in providing for poor families. Widowed mothers could now receive cash assistance under the Aid to Dependent Children program, and the unemployed found work with government-sponsored public works projects. The frightening economic and social deprivations of the depression convinced the majority of Americans that a social safety net was a worthy use of their tax dollars. These sentiments carried over to the 1960s when social reformers focused the public's attention on the millions of Americans still living in poverty. President Lyndon Johnson responded with the War on Poverty and the Great Society programs in 1964, significantly expanding welfare programs to include two-parent families, and adding new benefits such as food stamps, Medicaid, education subsidies, and job training.

More than thirty years later, critics contend that government welfare programs have been a wholesale failure, promoting illegitimacy, dependency, and an erosion of the work ethic. They point to statistics showing that government spending on poverty programs has increased enormously without causing a reduction in the poverty rate. Explains Michael Tanner, a researcher with the Cato Institute, "Before the beginning of the War on Poverty, the poverty rate declined dramatically. However, . . . by 1973 the poverty rate began to rise again. By 1995 the poverty rate had reached pre-1966 levels. . . . Spending per poor person has increased more than 700 percent since 1965. . . . In 1993 we spent more than $8,258 for every poor man, woman, and child in this country." Despite all this spending, according to the U.S. Census Bureau, 11.8 percent of the population, or 32.3 million people, were living below the poverty line in 1999.

The American public may not agree with all the negative characterizations of government welfare programs put forth by welfare's critics; however, it is clear that working- and middle-class Americans are running out of patience with government handouts. Since the 1970s, workers have seen their real wages stagnate, and increasingly, two incomes are necessary to maintain a middle-class lifestyle. Working mothers often feel resentment towards able-bodied mothers who would rather sit at home and collect welfare benefits than work for a living. Even welfare recipients are unsparing in their criticism of other recipients. Says one recipient interviewed by welfare researcher Karen Seccombe, "I think a lot of [people] are on [welfare] just to be on it. Lazy. Don't want to do nothing." There is a growing consensus that government welfare is fundamentally flawed because it does not distinguish between those who are temporarily down on their luck, the "deserving" poor, and those who simply refuse to work, the "undeserving" poor.

In place of government handouts, albeit with a few strings attached, the public has begun to embrace private organizations such as charities, churches, and businesses that provide training and employment resources as a more effective way to help the poor become self-sufficient. Private organizations may be partly supported with taxpayer dollars as state and local governments contract with them to administer welfare programs. Advocates argue, however, that private efforts, due to their limited budgets, have an incentive to eliminate waste and quickly screen out uncooperative candidates. Only those deserving of help will receive it, and the competitive nature of the free market will ensure that recipients are getting help that actually works. Whether private efforts can effectively replace government-run welfare programs and accomplish the claims of reformers is the subject of the following chapter.

"A private system of charity has all the advantages of a free market over government planning."

Private Charity Should Replace Welfare

David Kelley

David Kelley maintains in the following viewpoint that private charities have numerous advantages over welfare programs and can effectively replace the government's role in reducing poverty. According to Kelley, the independence of private agencies allows them to continually experiment with new approaches to helping the poor, unhindered by bureaucratic delays and political considerations. If the government were to eliminate its safety net for the poor, more money would remain in the economy to create entry-level jobs, and people would shift their giving from religious organizations and the arts to charities for the poor. Kelley is director of the Institute for Objectivist Studies, a center for research and education in the philosophy of objectivism.

As you read, consider the following questions:
1. According to Kelley, what makes charity effective in helping the poor?
2. Why do private agencies have a greater incentive to look for effective solutions to poverty, in the author's opinion?
3. What percentage of households, according to the author, contributed to charity in 1995?

Excerpted from *A Life of One's Own: Individual Rights and the Welfare State*, by David Kelley (Washington, DC: Cato Institute, 1998). Copyright © 1998 by the Cato Institute. Reprinted with permission.

Charity is the effort to help those in need. But need varies. Sometimes it is brief but intense, the product of an emergency like a hurricane or fire, and the victims need only temporary support to restore their normal, self-supporting lives. Other people are in need as a result of longer term mental or physical disabilities, and a longer term investment is necessary if they are to realize whatever potential they can. Need can arise from sheer bad luck, from factors truly outside the person's control; emergencies are once again the obvious example. At the other extreme, the straitened circumstances in which some people live are entirely their own doing, the result of abandoning responsibility for their lives. Most cases fall in between the extremes; poverty is the result of bad luck and bad choices in various degrees. As Alexis de Tocqueville observed, "Nothing is so difficult to distinguish as the nuances which separate unmerited misfortune from an adversity produced by vice. How many miseries are simultaneously the result of both these causes!"

For that reason, effective charity requires discrimination among cases and the use of measures adapted to the circumstances of the people one is trying to help. This was a central theme of 19th-century philanthropy. Relief workers in that era, especially in America, generally opposed government charity, like the British Poor Law, because it encouraged idleness, teaching the populace that income was possible without work. "Gratuitous aid," wrote New York charity worker John Griscom, produces a "relaxation of concern on the part of the poor to depend on their own foresight and industry." Many of the settlement houses and missions had "work tests"—men were expected to chop wood, women to sew, before they received meals or lodging—as a way of distinguishing freeloaders from people willing to take responsibility for themselves.

Governments find it extremely difficult to draw such distinctions. They simply provide benefits amounting to an alternative way of life for those at the bottom of the economic ladder, with no regard for merit and little regard for circumstance. Though welfare benefits hardly provide a comfortable existence, and benefit levels in some programs such as Aid to Families with Dependent Children (AFDC) had declined in real terms, the package of benefits in many states was more attractive than entry-level work. . . .

None of this is to say that a life on welfare is attractive. The welfare system is demeaning. It imposes on recipients every roadblock and indignity the bureaucratic mind can conceive. The problem is that both the benefits and the drawbacks fall upon the worthy and the unworthy alike. Government programs are unable to draw the distinctions necessary for effective charity because of four factors inherent in their nature *as* government programs:

1. If welfare is provided by the government in a modern liberal society, it must be construed as a right; it cannot depend on the personal virtues or vices of recipients or their willingness to take responsibility for themselves.

2. Since the state is the agency of coercion, its actions must be governed by the rule of law. Government bureaucrats cannot be given discretionary power to discriminate among recipients on the basis of personal morality or psychology.

3. As the agency of coercion, the government of a free country must also refrain from intruding into the personal dimensions of life, and this precludes the kind of active involvement often required for effective help.

4. Because government programs are bureaucratic and subject to the political process, they cannot have the flexibility to adapt to change, the spirit of innovation, and the diversity of approaches that private agencies have. . . .

Private agencies, by contrast, increasingly recognize the need to replace automatic help with contracts specifying terms that recipients must meet in order to receive help. This is especially true of shelters for the homeless, which deal with the toughest cases: many of the homeless are substance abusers who have been exploiting both public and private agencies—selling food stamps, getting free meals to conserve cash, and so forth—in order to obtain money for drugs and alcohol. At the Center for the Homeless in South Bend, Indiana, those seeking help must agree to abide by a strict set of rules; to receive any aid beyond the minimum, they must work with a case worker to create a plan for becoming self-sufficient. At Step 13 in Denver, those seeking shelter must agree to take Antabuse (a drug that causes sickness if one consumes alcohol) and submit to drug tests; and they can be expelled for disruptive behavior. Above and beyond the specific rationales for those rules, they convey the message that help is conditional, not an entitlement, and that irresponsibility will have consequences. . . .

Confronting Government's Shortcomings

For millennia, mankind has dreamed of banishing want and suffering from the world. Socialism promised the fulfillment of that ambition: the vast power of government would be harnessed to the purpose of eliminating poverty. . . .

We now know that this hope of governmentally imposed perfection is an illusion. For a century, antipoverty reformers around the globe have tried every variant of governmental power, from terror and mass murder to ponderous legislation. No utopia has been created; in most places, poverty has continued to grow. . . .

In spite of all the historical lessons in government's shortcomings, the supposition still lingers that government can succeed absolutely. "In a system of independent private charities," says the critic, "won't people fall through the cracks? Who is to make sure that everyone gets the help they need?"

Notice the underlying assumption: under a governmental system of care, no one falls through the cracks! Obviously, this idea did not come from empirical observation, from walking the streets and alleys of our cities and seeing nothing but happy, well-adjusted people. It springs from this primitive belief that government has the power to put everything right, if it would just try hard enough.

All systems of charity have cracks. Suffering, tragedy, and injustice will always be part of the human condition. Under a system of voluntary charity, millions will go without proper assistance—just as they do today under a half-trillion-dollar system of government care. The more important questions are: which system shows more promise of long-run improvement, and which treats individuals with the dignity they are due—a bureaucratic system based ultimately on force, or a personalized system based on generosity and persuasion?

James L. Payne, *Overcoming Welfare*, 1998.

To be sure, there are fads in private philanthropy, and there is waste. Some charities spend disproportionate amounts of money on fundraising, using the proceeds of one direct-mail campaign to pay for the next one. But there are published standards on fundraising costs that donors can use to compare the organizations soliciting their money, and the better charities far exceed those standards. Government programs, moreover, do not avoid the problem of a "patchwork of services" attributed to the private sector. Despite the existence of hundreds of government programs, some 40 percent of people living below the poverty line receive no government assistance.

Government programs are subject to the political process. Legislative majorities representing diverse interests and viewpoints must come to agreement before any change is possible. Social service bureaucracies are bound by administrative law, which requires complex rules and procedures for carrying out the legislature's intent. Diversity, flexibility, and innovation are the last things one could hope for under such conditions. As is the case with other enterprises run by government, service is slow and unresponsive to customers, wasteful, bureaucratic, and constantly influenced by political considerations. The problems with AFDC, for example, had been clear since the 1960s, and every administration since then had promised reform. But it took 30 years to get the first significant change in the program—the reforms of 1996—and even those are partial.

Private agencies, by contrast, can adapt more quickly to changing circumstances and to feedback about the success or failure of their efforts. They can adopt new ideas about how to provide aid most effectively without having to go through the federal budget process or being bound by administrative law. Because private agencies are separate and independent, each can go its own way, experimenting with new approaches without putting other agencies at risk; there is no need to find a single nationwide approach. The welfare reforms of 1996 gave states much more latitude to adopt different ways of providing benefits to the poor, and the states have already begun experimenting with some new approaches. But "the laboratory of democracy" provided by 50 states cannot compare with the experience to be gained through hundreds of thousands of private agencies, from local shelters and youth programs to nationwide charities.

In addition to the greater freedom that private agencies enjoy, they have a much greater incentive to look for solutions that work. Government programs are funded by taxes, and failure rarely results in a program's being cut; failure is more often used as an argument that more money is required. But a private agency must raise funds from donors who contribute voluntarily. Its donors are customers who want to see results and can take their money or their volunteer time elsewhere if an organization is not producing results.

In short, a private system of charity has all the advantages of a free market over government planning. It is now common knowledge that government planning does not work in the commercial realm. Why would we expect things to be different in the philanthropic realm?

The Promise of Private Aid

Despite the advantages of private over public programs for helping the poor, many people have expressed misgivings. One common argument among theorists is that charity must be government run because it is what economists call a "public good." If Person A wants to see Person B's poverty or suffering relieved, A can obtain that value if someone else helps B no less than if A helps B himself. This is one of the features of a public good: nonpayers aren't excluded from benefiting. Each of us thus has an incentive not to help the poor, in the expectation that others will help them, and if we all act on that incentive no help will be forthcoming. The only way out of that dilemma is collective provision, to which individuals are forced to contribute.

But it is irresponsible to want help given without any corresponding desire to help. Some people do behave that way, but not everyone; despite the logic of the public-goods argument, many people are moved by the countervailing logic of the old question, What if everyone did that? In 1995, for example, 68.5 percent of households contributed to charity, giving an average of $1,017. Nearly half the adult population (93 million people) did volunteer work. Volunteers in formal programs gave 15.7 billion hours, or the equivalent of 9.2 million full-time employees, with a value estimated at $201 billion. The poor, moreover, are not an indivisible pool of suffering that must be alleviated as a totality. It is individuals who are poor, and their plight usually makes the strongest claim on family members, neighbors, and others in the community who know them. A great deal of private charity is local in nature. In helping a given person in my community, I may be conferring unintended value on other community members who know or encounter him, but not on an entire society. Those other community members, moreover, are more likely to know me and thus be in a position to exert social pressure on me to contribute.

But will private, voluntary giving be enough? That is the first question raised whenever the proposal to privatize charity is put forward. The large private charities are often the most vehement in opposing cutbacks in government spending—understandably, since most of them receive a major portion of their funding from government contracts. "Private charity is built on the foundation of government welfare," argues an official of Catholic Charities USA, which gets more than half its funds from government. "We can do what we do because Government provides the basic safety net."

Governments at all levels currently spend about $350 billion on means-tested programs. Charitable giving by individuals, foundations, and corporations came to $144 billion in 1995, but only about $12 billion of that was for human services; another $13 billion was for health, a category that includes some services for the poor. Offsetting this huge disparity is the fact that many people give much more in time, as volunteers, than in money. In the category of human services, the value of volunteer time came to about $17 billion in 1995. Americans also spent 4.6 billion hours doing informal volunteer work—caring for an elderly or disabled person, helping a neighbor—with a value of perhaps $50 billion.

Even so, by the most generous estimates, private giving for the relief of poverty is well under 30 percent of government spending. Since it does not come close to matching government expenditures, how could it possibly replace them? But that hardly counts as an argument against privatization, for three major reasons. The first is that government causes a significant amount of the poverty it aims to relieve. . . . The package of benefits available to poor mothers typically has a higher value than the money they could earn in an entry-level job. A young mother who has grown up in a welfare family and never completed high school or held a job can easily be sidetracked from the working economy by the welfare system. In addition . . . government regulations such as the minimum wage, occupational licensing, and business restrictions keep the otherwise enterprising poor from helping themselves. Without those barriers to self-reliance, and without the subsidies that undermine the incentives for self-reliance, it stands to reason that many fewer people would be welfare dependents.

Second, a good deal of the money government spends on means-tested programs never reaches the poor. John Goodman of the National Center for Policy Analysis and others, for example, estimated that in 1992 the nonwelfare income of poor people was $94 billion short of the income necessary for them all to live at or above the poverty line. That is less than one-third of the money government spent to lift them out of poverty. The rest goes to the welfare bureaucracy, consultants, and others who administer the system. Of course it would not be possible simply to send that $94 billion to the poor without some administration, nor would that money eliminate poverty. Poverty is more often caused and sustained by behavioral problems than by strictly financial ones. Still, it is hard to believe that the advantages of private over public aid would not produce a considerable savings.

Third, by nationalizing the charity industry, the government has displaced private spending on the poor. The $300 billion that government spends is taken from the private economy. Some portion of that sum would otherwise be spent on goods and services that create new entry-level jobs, providing opportunities for the poor. And some portion would be contributed to charities. Sixty years of AFDC and 30 years of the Great Society programs have produced the expectation that government will provide an adequate safety net for the poor, and people have shifted their charitable giving to religion, the arts, and other areas. Although it is not possible to quantify this "crowding out" effect precisely, or to predict the amount of private giving that would be shifted to aid for the poor if welfare were privatized, historical research has provided a few hints.

In a detailed study of Indianapolis in the 1870s and 1880s, when government aid was reduced as part of a nationwide reaction against "outdoor relief," Stephen T. Ziliak found that private contributions increased by approximately the same amount. Figures from the 1930s are also illuminating. From 1930 to 1932, as the Great Depression deepened, both government and private spending on poverty relief increased sixfold. After Roosevelt's election, government spending continued to increase rapidly as new programs were introduced, but private spending declined rapidly as people assumed that responsibility had been shifted to the government.

At the same time, private charitable organizations shifted their efforts from poverty relief to other goals. At the New York Association for Improving the Condition of the Poor (AICP), for example, "Many families formerly cared for by AICP have been turned over completely to public relief departments." Thus it is not surprising that charitable giving today goes predominantly to religion and other objects, with human services receiving a relatively small portion. But there is every reason to believe that the proportions would change if government were not already spending so much in this area.

We do not know with any certainty what the result would be of leaving aid to the poor in private hands. We can't predict what ideas people will come up with to solve the problems they observe. One can certainly find grounds for pessimism. In his study of 19th-century Indianapolis, for example, Ziliak found that replacing government spending with private funds had no effect on the average spell of welfare dependence, nor on the number of people finding jobs and becoming self-supporting. Nevertheless, private agencies can provide aid on a conditional basis rather than as an entitlement, and thus more effectively encourage responsibility. They can draw distinctions on the basis of character and psychology, tailoring the help they provide in ways that the government cannot. They can intervene in the personal lives of recipients in ways that get to the root of problems but would be intrusive violations of freedom if done by government workers. And private agencies can be much more flexible, responsive to changing circumstances, experimental, and diverse than government bureaucracies.

Nor can we predict how much aid would be given in a private system, nor in what forms. Our point of departure, morally speaking, is not the needs of recipients but the generosity of donors. It is the donors who set the terms. Recipients do not own those who support them, and thus do not have a right that must be met, come what may. Those who would privatize poverty relief do not have the burden of showing that all poverty would be dealt with as effectively as it is today by government programs, although . . . that [is] extremely likely. The burden is on those who support government programs to show why they think the poor are *entitled* on altruistic grounds to the aid they are receiving.

Compassion and generosity are virtues, and the charitable help they prompt us to provide the less fortunate is, for most of us, a part of what it means to live in a civilized society. But compassion, generosity, and charity are not the sum of morality, nor even its core; and they are not duties that create entitlements on the part of recipients. The poor do not own the productive, nor are the latter obliged to sacrifice the pursuit of their own happiness in service to the poor. If individuals are truly ends in themselves, then charity is not a duty but a value we choose to pursue. Each of us has the right to choose what weight charity has among the other values in our lives, instead of having the government decide what proportion of our income to take for that end. And each of us has the right to choose the particular people, projects, or causes we wish to support, instead of having government make that decision for us.

> *"[Private charity] is increasingly substituting for adequate public provision, both in the benefits obtained by individuals and at the overall level of social policy."*

Private Charity Should Not Replace Welfare

Janet Poppendieck

In the following viewpoint, Janet Poppendieck maintains that the growth of reliance on private charity to provide basic services for the poor has eroded support for a more extensive government welfare system. Instead of preventing poverty by providing an adequate safety net, the proliferation of private charities has enabled the government to shed its responsibility for the poor. In Poppendieck's opinion, private charity is not an adequate substitute for the food, shelter, and income the government once provided to the poor as entitlements. The author is the director of the Hunter College Center for the Study of Family Policy in New York City.

As you read, consider the following questions:
1. What events in the early 1980s brought about a dramatic expansion of private charitable food programs, according to the author?
2. In Poppendieck's opinion, how is the resurgence of charity a symptom and a cause of society's failure to face up to poverty?
3. Why is reliance on small-scale charity programs problematic, in the author's opinion?

Excerpted from *Sweet Charity? Emergency Flood and the End of Entitlement*, by Janet Poppendieck (New York: Viking, 1998). Copyright © 1998 by Janet Poppendieck. Reprinted with permission.

E mergency food as we know it is largely a product of the last decade and a half. Such programs did not suddenly begin in 1980, of course. Soup kitchens, food pantries, and food banks all existed in the United States before the decade began, but they were generally small in size and relatively few in number. Then, in the early 1980s, a series of factors converged to bring about a sudden, dramatic expansion of private charitable food programs. A sharp recession, widely regarded as the deepest since the Great Depression, arrived to accelerate a long-term trend toward increasing unemployment and decreasing job security. This destruction of livelihoods coincided with steep cutbacks in federal social spending which aggravated a long-term decline in the purchasing power of public assistance. Homeless people became visible in many of the nation's large cities, and the "New Poor" turned to their churches and union locals for help. Existing kitchens and food pantries found themselves with ever longer lines at their doors, and new programs were hastily established to help meet this need. The term "emergency food," which had originally designated programs designed to respond to a "household food emergency," now took on the connotation of a societal emergency, a time-limited, urgent need for help, and Americans responded, as they always do, with energy and compassion. In New York City one hundred new emergency food programs opened their doors in 1983 alone. Food banks, which receive donations of unsalable food from corporations and pass them along to frontline kitchens and pantries, multiplied from about two dozen in 1980 to more than a hundred by the middle of the decade. Food rescue programs, which redistribute perishable and prepared foods, were not even invented until City Harvest in New York City came up with the idea in the early 1980s; by the end of the decade, there were enough such programs to form a national association called Foodchain.

Voluntary Efforts

When the economy improved for some Americans, it left behind a layer of people who continued to rely upon this private charitable assistance to get by. Emergency food programs did not wither away. Through upturns and downturns, expansions and contractions, accelerations and recessions, they grew in number and capacity, and gradually they invested in equipment, warehouses, trucks, computers, the whole infrastructure of provision. Today there are tens of thousands of emergency food programs in the United States, providing assistance, at least occasionally, to nearly a tenth of the population. In 1994, Second Harvest, the national organization of food banks, projected that programs affiliated with its member banks had provided food to some 25,970,000 "unduplicated" clients in the previous year, most of it through kitchens and pantries.

Literally millions of Americans support these programs with contributions of food, money, time, and effort. They bring bags of rice and jars of peanut butter to collection points in the church sanctuary or the local library, or drop a can in the barrel just outside the supermarket door. They pack grocery bags at food pantries. They prepare and serve meals at soup kitchens and deliver sandwiches to encampments of homeless people. They organize canned goods drives in their schools and Sunday schools, and send their youth groups and scout troops to help sort the proceeds at the food bank. They pick up leftovers from caterers and restaurants, from corporate dining rooms and campus cafeterias, and rush them in special thermal containers to soup kitchens and shelters. They "check out hunger" at their local supermarket counters and "dine out to help out" with their American Express cards. They "tee off against hunger" on their golf courses, and run against hunger in their marathons. It is an outpouring of compassion, both organized and individual, that would be the envy of most societies in human history: a "kinder, gentler nation" indeed.

Kinder, Less Just

Unfortunately, this kindness comes with a price tag. "I have found the world kinder than I expected, but less just," Samuel Johnson is said to have remarked. The same might be said of the popular response to poverty and hunger in America. It, too, is kinder but less just, not merely less just than I hoped or expected it would be, but less just than it was two decades ago. Poor people have lost—have been deprived of—rights to food, shelter, and income that were theirs twenty years ago. The Personal Responsibility and Work Opportunity Reconciliation Act of 1996 (PRWORA) and the end of welfare as we know it are only the culmination of a long, dreary process that has undermined the nation's fragile safety net. The erosion of the value of the minimum wage, a reduction in the purchasing power of public assistance, the decline in job security, and wave after wave of cutbacks in food assistance, housing subsidies, and welfare benefits have all reduced the overall share of income going to the bottom layers of our society, and curtailed the legally enforceable claims that people in need may make upon the collectivity. Measurable inequality is more pronounced now than it has been at any point since World War II.

The growth of kindness and the decline in justice are intimately interrelated. In one direction, the relationship is obvious. Visit nearly any soup kitchen or food pantry in America and you will find its staff and volunteers gearing up to cope with the sharp increases in need that they anticipate as the PRWORA—"welfare reform"—gradually takes effect. The cutbacks and reductions in public assistance benefits, along with declining wages at the bottom of the pay scale, increasing shelter costs, and a growing reliance on layoffs and downsizing to increase profitability are reducing people to destitution and sending them to the food lines. These changes are causing the hunger to which kindhearted people are responding with pantries and kitchens.

Private Charity Normalizes Poverty

It works the other way too, however, and this is less obvious. The resurgence of charity is at once a *symptom* and a *cause* of our society's failure to face up to and deal with the erosion of equality. It is a symptom in that it stems, in part at least, from an abandonment of our hopes for the elimination of poverty; it signifies a retreat from the goals as well as the means that characterized the Great Society. It is symptomatic of a pervasive despair about actually solving problems that has turned us toward ways of managing them: damage control, rather than prevention. More significantly, and more controversially, the proliferation of charity *con-*

tributes to our society's failure to grapple in meaningful ways with poverty. My argument, in short, is that this massive charitable endeavor serves to relieve pressure for more fundamental solutions. It works pervasively on the cultural level by serving as a sort of "moral safety valve"; it reduces the discomfort evoked by visible destitution in our midst by creating the illusion of effective action and offering us myriad ways of participating in it. It creates a culture of charity that normalizes destitution and legitimates personal generosity as a response to major social and economic dislocation.

It works at the political level, as well, by making it easier for government to shed its responsibility for the poor, reassuring policymakers and voters alike that no one will starve. By harnessing a wealth of volunteer effort and donations, it makes private programs appear cheaper and more cost effective than their public counterparts, thus reinforcing an ideology of voluntarism that obscures the fundamental destruction of rights. And, because food programs are logistically demanding, their maintenance absorbs the attention and energy of many of the people most concerned about the poor, distracting them from the larger issues of distributional politics. It is not an accident that poverty grows deeper as our charitable responses to it multiply.

If emergency food were only a kindly add-on to an adequate and secure safety net of public provision, I would have no problem with it. It would reach some poor people who are ineligible for public programs, or unwilling or unable to avail themselves of such welfare provisions. It would provide a few extras for people whose wages or pensions or public assistance payments leave them little margin for error or enjoyment. It would serve as an invitation and inducement to people to seek the help of programs designed to meet more complex needs—to provide education, job training, health care screening, or mental health services, for example—and it would reduce the operating costs of congregate meal programs for senior citizens and the food expenditures of daycare centers, freeing resources for enrichment programs. It would tide people over in the unpredictable emergencies that can strike anyone without warning, and assist whole communities confronted with floods, hurricanes, and other natural disasters. And it would provide constructive outlets for food that might otherwise go to waste, both government surpluses and corporate products. As a supplement to a robust array of constructive public provisions, emergency food (renamed community food security, or supplemental food) would clearly be a net social gain, and we could all rejoice in the energy and compassion of the volunteers and the generosity of donors that make possible a kinder, gentler society.

Eroding the Safety Net

If, however, as I believe, charity food is increasingly substituting for adequate public provision, both in the benefits obtained by individuals and at the overall level of social policy, then it is time to take a closer look at the costs of kindness. What accounts for the dramatic expansion and enduring popularity of emergency food programs? Why do people use them, and why do other people provide the resources to support them? How did this phenomenon get started, and what keeps it growing? How does it affect the people who use it, and what is its impact upon the larger culture and society? Does it constitute an additional resource for poor people, or does it contribute to the erosion and destruction of the public safety net, substituting for rather than expanding upon public provisions? These are the questions that [must be answered] . . . to understand the larger dynamic by which we have allowed ourselves to be diverted from the task of eliminating hunger and reducing inequality.

Replacing Basic Social Provisions

The emergency food phenomenon is indicative of a larger social trend. A growing reliance on small-scale, local, grassroots, voluntary programs is not restricted to poverty. It has characterized recent response to a host of other social ills, as well: AIDS, battered women, illiteracy, and child abuse come readily to mind as examples. There are undoubtedly others, because the same frustrations with government and the same despair over the potential for humane, effective public policy underlie civic response to many pressing problems. I am not claiming that these vernacular efforts are the only responses, but that these are the responses that have captured the public imagination, and, as the April 1997 "Summit" on volunteering reveals with startling clarity, these are the approaches that are being promoted by the nation's official leaders—presidents, generals, and the like. At first glance, many of these projects are heartwarming expressions of neighborly solidarity, compassion, and caring. They are not problematic, in and of themselves. They become problematic when we use them in place of the basic social provisions that any complex industrial or postindustrial society needs. Tutoring programs are good, but they are not a substitute for good schools. Friendly visitors for AIDS patients are good, but they are no substitute for medical care or access to pharmaceuticals. Volunteer advocates for abused children are good, but they can not replace adequately staffed and accountable systems of foster care, and should not replace social supports that enable families to stay together in times of stress and crisis. . . .

Charity Versus Entitlement

Emergency food programs illustrate the retreat to charity especially well because they offer such pronounced contrast to the food assistance policies and politics of the previous two decades. In the late 1960s, this country experienced a "rediscovery" of hunger in America. It began when a U.S. Senate committee decided to hold hearings on the operation of federal anti-poverty programs in Mississippi. Civil rights worker Marian Wright (now Marian Wright Edelman), who would later go on to found and direct the Children's Defense Fund, convinced some of the visiting senators, among them Bobby Kennedy, to accompany her on a tour of the back roads and empty cupboards of the Mississippi Delta. Many counties in the Delta had recently switched from the distribution of federal surplus commodities, which were free, to the newly revived Food Stamp Program which required the purchase of stamps. Delta sharecroppers, unneeded and unemployed as the mechanical cotton picker took over their jobs, were unable to scrape together the cash to purchase the stamps, and without the commodities, they were slowly starving. In fact, civil rights activists charged that the changeover to food stamps had been undertaken precisely to drive economically obsolete but politically aroused blacks out of the Delta. The senators encountered hunger and malnutrition in their starkest forms. In 1967, nearly anything Bobby Kennedy did was news, and hunger in Mississippi became news in America. . . .

Charity Precludes Concrete Action

It is well-known to social scientists that those nations which provide generous social welfare systems know little of homelessness, hunger, poverty, or high rates of violent crime. The only response Americans (of conservative, moderate, or liberal stripe) tend to muster to this information is comments such as, "Aren't the taxes too high there?" or "Aren't the governments too strong?" Suddenly, when asked to potentially express "love" through concrete financial action, a new reticence takes over. "Let's not get carried away."

Policy experts have long debated America's lack of a strong social welfare system, usually the rubric of "American exceptionalism." To the many causes for the historic weakness of the American welfare state, I note that in addition to the usual explanations—heterogeneity of our country by nationality, ethnicity, and religion; individualism and a cowboy settler mentality; and the weakness of trade unionism, socialism, and labor parties—the meagerness of the American public social welfare system is also explained by our love affair with charity, voluntarism, and nonprofit organization. America's private system of organization of social services, universities, hospitals, and other health care facilities is a brake upon any effort to construct a fairer, better society. As was evident in the health care debate several years ago, private parties are so strong in America that even mild reforms are often scotched. In addition to the raw political power of both the nonprofit sector and the private for-profit sector . . . , there is the power of the charitable ideology. A combination of charity, therapy, and correction is held to be necessary in the United States to solve a host of social problems. Some descriptors (the aged, a homeless woman and child) conjure up the romance of charity, while others (the drug user, the male vagrant) conjure up correctional strategies, and some (such as mental illness or children who are insufficiently passive and submissive in school) suggest some modicum of therapy and correction. But very few people favor delivering cash to people in need.

David Wagner, *What's Love Got to Do with It?* 2000.

In the aftermath of the hunger revelations of the late 1960s, an anti-hunger movement emerged, and it proved particularly adept at using the tools of legislation, litigation, and community organization to bring pressure on Congress to reform federal food assistance programs. In the late 1960s and early 1970s the "hunger lobby," as the anti-hunger network was quickly labeled, scored victory after victory, reforming existing food assistance programs and devising new ones. Federal expenditures on food assistance grew, in real (inflation adjusted) dollars, by 500 percent in the decade following the rediscovery of hunger. When this decade of achievement began, it was not immediately obvious to all that food stamps were preferable to surplus commodities. After all, it was the purchase requirement in food stamps that accounted for the severest malnutrition exposed in the Mississippi Delta. Gradually, however, as purchase requirements were reduced—and eliminated for the poorest households—and benefits were increased to ensure access to a nutritionally adequate if minimal diet, the advantages of food stamps became clear. They eliminated much of the hardship and inconvenience of the commodity program, in which recipients often had to carry home a month's supply at a time—a month's supply of whatever happened to be in surplus at the moment. Food stamps permitted their recipients to shop with the same convenience and almost the same degree of consumer choice as their non-poor neighbors. In a society in which the consumer role is of paramount importance, they "mainstreamed" participants, making their lives, or at least their grocery shopping trips, as much as possible like those of their non-poor neighbors.

To me, these characteristics made food stamps good social policy, not only from an efficiency and cost-effectiveness standpoint, but also because the program promoted social integration. It helped to bring us together, to make us one society. I was taken aback, therefore, when soup kitchens and food pantries began to proliferate in the early 1980s. They looked to me like a great leap backward. In the first place, they seemed to embody approaches to hunger that were precisely the opposite of those that had animated the anti-hunger agenda of the seventies. They were a retreat from the effort at mainstreaming and inclusion, however imperfect, represented by food stamps to programs that separated and segregated poor people. They were a retreat from the convenience and consumer choice of stamps and vouchers to the predetermined menu of provisions in kind. They were a retreat from national standards to haphazard local provision. Most important, they were a retreat from rights to gifts. Poor people might be, and often are, very well treated in charitable emergency food programs, but they have no rights, at least no legally enforceable rights, to the benefits that such programs provide. In a very real sense, emergency food seemed to threaten not only a reversal of the hard-won victories of the anti-hunger movement of the sixties and seventies but also a retreat to the reliance on private charity that characterized American society before the New Deal.

*"Emerging reports prove that [churches] . . .
succeed in combating social problems."*

Religious Organizations Can Reduce Poverty

Ronald J. Sider

The 1996 welfare reform bill includes a Charitable Choice provision that allows churches and other faith-based organizations (FBOs) to contract with state governments to administer welfare programs in their communities, as long as beneficiaries are not required to participate in religious activities. President George W. Bush has plans to expand Charitable Choice to allow FBOs to play a greater role in providing assistance to the needy. Ronald J. Sider contends in the following viewpoint that FBOs can succeed in reducing poverty where government welfare programs have failed by providing moral guidance, a sense of family, and links to jobs and other resources within their communities. According to the author, FBOs can raise funds through private donations to support the religious component of their outreach. Sider is a professor of theology and culture at Eastern Seminary.

As you read, consider the following questions:

1. According to the author, what assumptions about people and their environment have driven social policy in the last few decades?
2. What special strengths do churches offer the poor, in Sider's opinion?
3. In the author's opinion, how can religious discrimination be avoided when funding churches to provide services to the poor?

From "Revisiting Mt. Carmel Through Charitable Choice," by Ronald J. Sider, *Christianity Today*, June 11, 2001. Copyright © 2001 by Christianity Today, Inc. Reprinted with permission.

It is time for a nonviolent return to Mt. Carmel. In Elijah's time, most Israelites had forsaken Yahweh to worship Baal, so Elijah challenged the prophets of Baal to a public confrontation on Mt. Carmel. Elijah proposed that both he and the prophets of Baal place a slaughtered bull on an altar and then each call on his god to send down fire to devour the sacrifice. "The god who answers by fire is indeed God" (1 Kings 18:24, NRSV). The prophets of Baal failed, but Yahweh's heavenly fire consumed Elijah's drenched sacrifice.

Challenging the Secularists

Today two competing worldviews and two competing views of persons offer different solutions to our social problems. Naturalists say that nature is all that exists and people are just complex socioeconomic machines—therefore all you have to do to end poverty or correct societal dysfunction is adjust the external environment, modify the economic incentives, and change the educational inputs. Much social policy in the last few decades worked with this assumption. But if historic biblical theism is true, should we not expect social programs combining spiritual and social transformation to work better than either purely secular or nominally religious programs?

President Bush's forming of a White House Office on Faith-Based and Community Initiatives (OFBCI) continues to generate controversy, even in Christian circles, but I believe it gives us an opportunity for a nonviolent reenactment of Elijah's contest with the false prophets.

Let's challenge the secularists to a test. Let's invite our best secular universities to have their top social scientists conduct careful, sophisticated comparative evaluations of at least three types of social-service providers: the secular, the religiously affiliated, and the holistic Christian that combine evangelism, prayer, and dependence on the Holy Spirit with the best of the medical and social sciences. (In fact, why not also include Buddhist and Muslim programs?) The programs could be job training, drug and alcohol rehabilitation—whatever. The only significant variable would be the absence or presence of faith-based components grounded in the biblical belief that people need spiritual as well as socioeconomic renewal.

Ram Cnaan, professor of social work at the University of Pennsylvania, points out in the important new book *The Newer Deal: Social Work and Religion in Partnership* that government, many in the media, and philanthropic foundations endorse a major expansion of faith-based organizations' role in delivering social services, in struggling against poverty and urban social decay, and in promoting new partnerships between these religious institutions and other sectors of society. The new White House office, with Catholic scholar John J. DiIulio Jr. as its director, is only the most visible example of sweeping societal change.

Employing Churches to Combat Social Problems

There are a number of reasons for the growing interest in faith-based organizations.

First, the government has reduced its support for social services during the last two decades; thus other societal sectors have had to fill the gap.

Second, neither the liberal nor conservative solutions tried thus far to solve our enormous social problems have worked adequately. The richest nation in history has persistent, widespread poverty—in 1999, 32.3 million Americans found themselves below the poverty level and 44 million without health insurance. Not all antipoverty government programs have failed, of course. Many, including Social Security, the Earned Income Tax Credit (EITC), and the Women, Infants, and Children nutrition program, succeeded. But poverty, violence, and social disorder still flourish at the hearts of our great cities.

"No one has a clue as to what it would take for public policy, to be sufficient," former U.S. Sen. Daniel P. Moynihan acknowledged in a speech at Harvard just a few years ago. Partly out of desperation, policy experts and the public generally began to wonder if religious groups had at least more of the answer. Today, Cnaan says, "the public is ready to have government support the religious community in doing what everyone else has failed to do."

Third, a growing body of research demonstrates that religion often goes hand in hand with good citizenship and overall health. Scholars as diverse as psychiatrist David Larson, for years a policy analyst at the U.S. Department of Health and Human Services, Patrick F. Fagan at the Heritage Foundation, and Cnaan cite a wide range of studies showing that "religion is strongly associated with good citizenship and improved physical and mental health." Active participation in a religious group correlates with lower suicide rates, drug use, and criminal behavior; better health; and altruistic behavior. Independent Sector's 1994 survey found that persons who attend church weekly are about twice as likely to volunteer (and volunteer twice as many hours) as nonchurchgoers. Catholic University of America sociologist Dean R. Hoge recently concluded, "Church attendance and participation in church programs are by far the strongest predictors of volunteering." In a widely cited study, Harvard economist Richard Freeman found that church attendance was the best predictor of which young inner-city black males were likely to escape the syndrome of gangs, drugs, and prison.

Emerging reports prove that faith-based organizations (FBOs) succeed in combating social problems. Graduates of Teen Challenge have an 85 percent drug rehabilitation success rate, according to a recent Northwestern University study—in contrast with another study's finding of a 28 percent rate for secular programs. Faith-based mentoring teams seem to have played a crucial role in enabling Ottawa County in Michigan to become the first county in the United States to have nobody on the welfare rolls. Lawndale Community Center's faith-based health center has helped cause a 60 percent drop in infant mortality rates in a destitute section of Chicago, prompting headlines in local papers and careful exploration by federal health officials.

Too much of the evidence is still anecdotal. We need far more extensive scholarly evaluation of holistic faith-based providers. But there are enough indicators to raise the possibility that holistic FBOs sometimes succeed when almost everything else has failed.

Moral and Spiritual Transformation

Fourth, there is growing agreement that our social problems have both socioeconomic and moral/religious roots and that therefore moral and spiritual transformation must be a part of the solution. Economists Sheldon Danziger and Peter Gottschalk report a fascinating analysis in their book *America Unequal*. They ask how much of the growing poverty from 1973 to 1991 is due to economic factors (especially declining wages for low-skilled persons) and how much is due to the rapid growth of single-parent families. Their answer? The two factors are almost equally important. A child who grows up in a single-parent family is 11 times more likely to experience persistent poverty than a child who grows up with both parents. Obviously, structural economic factors have contributed to the decline of two-parent families, but so have changing ethical norms and personal moral choices. Equally obvious is that if we want to reverse the decline of two-parent families, our churches will have to play the leading role.

Fifth, Cnaan says that religious communities are already providing social services for their surrounding communities "to a degree unimagined and unacknowledged in the social work literature." In his study of six different cities, he found that each congregation provided direct and indirect support for social programs (mostly for persons outside their own congregation) worth over $144,000 per year. If the congregations he studied are typical and his calculations correct, that would mean the nation's congregations annually contribute about $36 billion for the needy.

Offering Special Strengths

Churches offer special strengths. Serving the poor is a central part of many congregations' self-defined mission; they have a semiorganized pool of volunteers; during the week, they provide physical space; they can raise discretionary funds; they have a place and authority to assemble the community for discussion; they have the potential for political influence; they offer moral authority and evidence that people can leave behind destructive behavior; they provide a sense of family that can substitute for dysfunctional family life; and they have links to a larger community that can offer jobs, resources, and political influence. Finally, they are present—almost everywhere.

One study of four Los Angeles neighborhoods discovered

on average 35 religious congregations and 12.5 religiously affiliated nonprofits per square mile. That is more than all the gasoline stations, liquor stores, and supermarkets in these neighborhoods combined. Gallup polls reveal that seven of every ten Americans say they are members of a church or synagogue, and four of ten attend worship at least once a week. Especially in inner-city neighborhoods where almost every other institution has failed or disappeared, the very presence of religious congregations almost everywhere is an enormous strength.

None of this suggests that religious congregations can replace all government programs. If the 325,000 churches, synagogues, and mosques were to replace government funds just for the four basic anti-poverty programs (Temporary Assistance for Needy Families, EITC, Supplemental Security Income, and food stamps), each congregation would have to add $289,000 to its annual budget. If congregations included the federal share of Medicaid, the figure would jump to $612,000. That would be difficult since, according to sociologist Mark Chaves, the median annual budget for all congregations is less than $60,000.

Church-State Hurdles and Secular Bias

A complex set of problems clusters around the issues of separation of church and state and religious tolerance. For private foundations, of course, the church-state issue is a pseudoproblem. For governments, I think the charitable-choice legislation and the OFBCI's policies offer a clear, workable path that the Supreme Court will uphold.

But the problem is much deeper. In this highly pluralistic society, there are many different religious groups with divergent beliefs in every community. Do nonreligious funders endorse particular religious doctrines and practices if they fund the social services of such groups? The obvious answer is no. Sometimes, however, people feel otherwise. I remember a pious relative of mine who refused to vote because he thought that would mean a commitment to everything that the politician did. I disagree. Funding, like voting, implies a limited endorsement of specific activities and outcomes.

The core of the problem, however, lies still deeper. Two

different worldviews and understandings of persons compete today: historic Christian theism and naturalism.

Many FBOs work self-consciously within the worldview of historic Christian theism. I am just completing a multi-year study of selected churches in the greater Philadelphia area, and it is clear many of them will not accept funds if doing so would lead them to weaken the faith component in their social-service programs.

These agencies seek spiritual transformation in their clients not only as a worthy goal in itself but also as fundamental to achieving social-improvement goals. The faith-based approach of these agencies is grounded in an understanding of persons as free body-soul unities created in the image of God. In this worldview, no area of a person's life can be considered adequately in isolation from the spiritual. Strong faith introduces and strengthens an ethical framework that discourages destructive social behavior. Personal faith in Christ brings a powerful liberation from enervating feelings of guilt and failure, as well as a supernatural power that transforms believers, enabling them to live differently. Faith in Christ provides an inner energy that goes beyond drug addicts' ability to say no to drugs and yes to family responsibilities.

Further, the community of believers offers a network of caring friends who provide emotional, spiritual, and material support. For all these reasons, many Christian agencies believe that an integrated, holistic approach that embraces the best of the medical and social sciences but also seeks to nurture people in a right relationship with God yields more effective social services.

This approach contrasts with the naturalistic worldview that has dominated the academic world, media elites, and policy circles for decades. As Carl Sagan and others have argued, nature is all that exists and science is the only avenue to knowledge. Glenn Loury has summarized this view as saying people are "soulless creatures"; therefore, technical, professional knowledge and skills are sufficient to address social problems. The way to eliminate negative social behavior and reduce poverty is to change the environment, modify the economic incentives, or apply a medical or therapeutic treatment regimen. Naturalists maintain that reference to a spiritual dimension is irrelevant to the task of solving social problems. According to Christian FBOs, however, such an approach does not address the whole person, and thus can only get at part of the problem.

The Progress of Charitable Choice

The government and faith community collaborations that Charitable Choice has encouraged have already produced important benefits. New financial relationships have begun, but also new non-financial forms of collaboration. The traditional social services network is being broadened and energized through the inclusion of new helpers.

And these fresh troops are doing many new things. Many congregations have started providing social services that even they had not previously attempted. Specifically, many have moved from "commodity-based benevolence" (operating food pantries and used clothing centers) to "relational" ministry—working intensively with needy families, face-to-face, for months. While our survey uncovered collaborations on a wide variety of social services like child care, transportation, drug rehabilitation, homeless services, English courses, and parenting classes, the most common initiatives were mentoring and job training programs that involved extensive personal contact between poor individuals and their religious helpers. This is the most important "added value" that religious organizations bring to poverty relief.

Moving welfare recipients to independence requires intensive labor. Most of the women making the transition need individualized emotional and practical support, something government caseworkers rarely provide. Caring volunteers from faith-based organizations, on the other hand, can and do provide tremendous personal assistance, encouragement, and accountability to poor families moving off the dole. Some religious groups are even well-positioned to handle "hard-to-serve" clients who require specialized attention, tough love, hope, and spiritual motivation if they are to successfully change their lives.

Amy Sherman, "A Survey of Church-Government Anti-Poverty Partnerships," *American Enterprise*, June 2000.

Alan Wolfe's study in *One Nation After All* reveals that Americans tend to interpret any bold public expressions of religion as distasteful impositions on other people's religious rights. The invitation to saving faith in Jesus Christ issues from an authoritative claim about the uniqueness of Christ that many find restrictive and exclusive. Thus, despite the resurgence of interest in religion, the notion of inviting others to adopt a specific religious belief, especially if it contains an exclusive claim to truth, is countercultural in American society today. Nonreligious funders may overlook a perfunctory prayer to start the day, but they often refuse to support holistic social programs run by Christians who think that encouraging the adoption of a specific religious faith is an essential component of their social program.

Choosing Tolerance and Equity

Tolerance, of course, can be fully compatible with vigorous disagreement. The only genuinely tolerant position welcomes all voices, including those claiming that some other voices are wrong. If they are to be truly tolerant, nonreligious funders can and should fund social-service providers grounded in mutually exclusive worldviews, as long as all providers demonstrate that they are successfully producing the desired public goods and respect the freedom of others, even as they disagree with them.

The only way not to discriminate against a religious perspective is to provide equal benefits to all service providers of every and no religious faith, if they can demonstrate that their programs are producing the desired public goods (successful job training, drug rehabilitation, and so on). Nonreligious funders can, of course, fund parts of the programs of deeply religious FBOs without funding their inherently religious activities.

The charitable-choice legislation (recently endorsed by the National Association of Evangelicals) protects both the religious freedom of participants and the religious integrity of FBOs. Section 104 of the 1996 Welfare Bill specifies that government funds not be used for "inherently religious" activities, which it defines as "sectarian worship, instruction, or proselytization." FBOs, however, can raise private money to fund these inherently religious activities as long as it is clear that government does not sponsor these activities and clients are not required to participate against their will. FBOs should not use government grants to pay for staff time devoted to specifically religious activities. If a staff position commingles religious and nonreligious activities so that making clear distinctions becomes problematic, then the FBO should choose to fund this staff position entirely from private donations, without limiting government funding for the rest of the program.

The Charitable Choice legislation also specifies that agencies not select or reject clients on the basis of religion and that participants must have a secular option, freely choose a religious provider, and be allowed to opt out of the inherently religious activities. These guidelines can be adopted by both governments and private, secular donors as they fund FBOs.

Two-Sided Challenge

Let's respectfully but confidently and pointedly invite the secular academic world and secular foundations funding social services to a rigorous public test. We need not mention Mt. Carmel. We need only insist that for the sake of pursuing knowledge (so we learn more about what works, what does not work, and why) and for the sake of efficiency in using societal funds to combat social problems, theists and naturalists ought to join together in a grand, thorough, comparative evaluation.

We have a few studies like that of Teen Challenge, plus a lot of powerful stories of dramatic transformation. But as DiIulio likes to say, the plural of anecdote is not data. Fortunately, DiIulio has promised to encourage more objective evaluation of all types of programs.

Christians should dare major nonreligious donors to fund a wide range of providers, both religious and secular; insist on careful record-keeping and participation in scholarly studies as part of the grant; and fund the sophisticated sociological studies.

At the same time, evangelicals should be challenged.

Faith-based agencies must be willing to open their programs and records to rigorous analysis and careful record-keeping. Some evangelical organizations hesitate to accept this careful scrutiny. What do we have to fear? Do we secretly doubt the power of the gospel? Or are our records (financial and otherwise) so sloppy that we fear exposure? If the latter, let's get them in shape.

Fortunately, we have a whole generation of outstanding evangelical scholars who can participate, along with the most hard-nosed academic agnostics, in the necessary evaluations. We need not fear that subtle or hidden secular biases in the methodology will skew the results.

Would it not be stunning if a decade from now we could point to study after study concluding that, other things being equal, holistic faith-based social-service providers combining prayer, Bible study, and sensitive evangelism with the best of the medical and social sciences consistently produced better results than secular or nominally religious providers? Philosophical naturalists would have to rethink their concepts of human nature.

I have no anxiety about the outcome if the contest occurs. What frightens me is that the invitation may arrive and Christians will fail to show.

Awakening to an Opportunity

In a real sense, the basic invitation has been sent already. The policy elites have already acknowledged that the secular solutions tried before have not been adequate. They have already invited faith-based agencies to play an expanded, central role. The OFBCI may soon announce a massive rollout of mentoring programs already begun by DiIulio in Philadelphia. To answer that call, we will need millions of Christian volunteers and billions of dollars in additional donations—because the government dare not fund the specifically religious activities that are so central to holistic FBOs.

Do enough Christians care? Or has materialism so hardened our hearts that most Christians will sleep through one of the most amazing opportunities in our history?

Let's be very clear. The present window of opportunity will not remain open for long. If in five years large numbers of Christians have not stepped forward to answer the call for expanded faith-based programs solving our toughest social problems, policy elites will say "Been there, done that."

They will turn elsewhere for solutions, concluding that Christians did not even care enough to test their own claim that people need both Jesus and a job.

Perhaps the real test will be not whether historic theism works better than naturalism, but whether Christians practice what Jesus teaches about the poor.

"[Private companies and government] can develop a competitive marketplace to place disenfranchised workers."

Privatization of Welfare Benefits Recipients

Peter Cove

Peter Cove is the founder of America Works, a private company that has contracted with state governments to move welfare recipients off the welfare rolls and into full-time jobs. In the following viewpoint, Cove asserts that his company has placed hard-to-serve welfare recipients in jobs that pay above the minimum wage. In addition, America Works has increased the job retention rates of welfare recipients by placing them at companies for a paid, four-month, on-the-job training period. Cove contends that government must become less bureaucratic and take more responsibility for the successes and failures of its private contractors, rewarding only the programs that get people jobs.

As you read, consider the following questions:

1. According to Cove, what percentage of welfare recipients who find jobs through America Works remain off the welfare rolls three years later?
2. How does the Supported Work program increase job retention among welfare recipients, in the author's opinion?
3. In Cove's opinion, how does the impact of free market forces make government a more competitive player in the successes and failures of its private contractors?

Excerpted from Peter Cove's testimony before the House Small Business Committee, Subcommittee on Empowerment, May 25, 1999.

M y name is Peter Cove. I am the founder of America Works, a private for-profit welfare-to-work company with seven offices nation-wide. America Works currently serves welfare recipients in four States out of offices in New York City, the Bronx, Westchester County, and Albany, New York; Baltimore, Maryland; Indianapolis, Indiana; and Miami, Florida. We will open four more offices this year, in Oakland, California; Dallas, Texas; Atlanta, Georgia; and Washington, DC. In the future, we look forward to the opportunity to place welfare recipients in Chicago, Los Angeles, as well as in many other vital American cities. Since opening our doors in 1984, America Works has removed over 15,000 people from the welfare roles by placing them in full-time jobs. As we expand, soon America Works will place that many welfare recipients each year. . . .

Finding Jobs for Welfare Recipients

America Works places the hard-to-serve welfare population and has jobs for all skill levels. The average Temporary Assistance for Needy Families (TANF) recipient that we successfully place has been on welfare for 5 years and scores academically at the 8th grade level. Half do not have a GED/high school diploma. The New York State Department of Labor has determined that 88% of the people placed by America Works remain off the welfare rolls three years later. Our Supported Work model is largely responsible for this success rate.

America Works pioneered the now nationally adopted work-first approach to welfare reduction. Clients first participate in up to four weeks of training, focusing on soft skills like communication, getting along, developing a positive attitude and overcoming fears. We prepare clients for interviews, let them brush up on clerical or non-clerical skills, match them with job openings and arrange interviews with potential employers. America Works' Job Readiness services prepare participants for jobs with the specific companies at which we place, with curricula geared to the specific soft and hard skills that our employers demand. America Works tailors its 4-week curriculum to the unique training procedures and needs of selected employers thereby giving our participants a competitive advantage when competing against outside applicants for positions.

Employer relationships and intensive follow up support are two key elements of our Supported Work model. America Works' ability to use a seasoned private sector sales force to get participants quickly into jobs separates us from the competition. Companies want to work with us and want to hire our TANF clients. Sales Representatives compete amongst each other to place participants in well-suited jobs, with performance bonuses awarded to Sales Representatives who consistently make placements that work and last.

Nationwide, America Works places participants in a wide range of clerical and non-clerical positions, at an average nation-wide starting salary of $8.50/hour. Each office brings in over 50 new position openings per week and places over 20 participants per week. Having many jobs and a wide variety of jobs allows us to place people carefully according to their skills and their interests, a strategy that translates into higher long-term retention rates.

Supported Work

Clients are placed at companies for up to a four-month training period, called Supported Work. Supported Work is a countable work activity under TANF regulations, like On the Job Training (OJT) or Work Experience. Supported Work allows us to provide 4 months of training at no additional cost. During Supported Work, companies pay participants an hourly wage, thereby matching funds provided through government contracts. During Supported Work, America Works is the employer, which allows us to play a hands-on role during the crucial initial training period. This extra support up front improves our retention rates in the long run, by getting the welfare recipient off to a strong start. Supported Work typically lasts for four months, after which unsubsidized employment is secured at the same site. Not every participant engages in Supported Work; some go directly on to the company payroll in unsubsidized positions, if the company requests it.

After completing the Supported Work trial period, the candidates are hired permanently onto companies' payrolls.

Companies sign contracts with America Works stating that each participant with a satisfactory performance record will be hired into an unsubsidized position at the end of the Supported Work period, at the companies' discretion.

A personalized Case Manager mentors candidates on personal and professional issues, by visiting them and their supervisors on the job and meeting with them during non-working hours. This allows America Works to continuously assess the job match to ensure it is ideal, and provide clients with additional support services as required. The Case Manager acts as an advocate, partner, mentor and supervisor, helping candidates confront the challenges to entering the workforce, whether professional or personal. The Case Manager works with a small caseload of 20 participants, allowing them to provide clients with intensive and cohesive one-on-one counseling. Case Managers also help coordinate social services with work obligations, making sure that clients receive the counseling and services necessary to ensure long-term workplace success. Case Managers continue to counsel and assist clients for an additional 6 months once unsubsidized employment is obtained, and indefinitely as needed.

Job Retention and Advancement

The America Works Case Manager meets at least once per week with each participant. The Case Manager makes work site visits and conducts evaluations with the on-site supervisor, coaching the participant on workplace skills and behaviors. In addition, the Case Manager coordinates the provision of social services . . . during non-working hours, monitoring attendance and personal improvements. The key to the success of our case-management retention services is that the same coach monitors success both on the job and off, providing a level of continuity while teaching TANF recipients how to manage the demands of the workplace with the competing demands of their home and personal lives.

This method is the reason why America Works ensures at least 6 months of retention at unsubsidized jobs—support is consistent and integrated. The wisdom of this strategy is proven by retention statistics yet to be paralleled by any of our competitors.

America Works recognizes that the barriers to employment among TANF recipients are often daunting and debilitating. For this reason, America Works collaborates with a range of social service providers who tend to the wide variety of client needs. In addition, America Works ensures that those supportive services are coordinated with the work schedule of participants.

America Works likes to make sure that participants realize growth opportunities by urging them to continually develop improved work and personal skills. The majority of the positions in which we place participants offer room for growth and advancement.

In addition, America Works' Case Managers encourage participants to take advantage of training and educational opportunities available in their communities to improve their market value for future advancements and salary increases. Historically, those programs have included GED, English as a Second Language (ESL), college credits, and vocational training. We enroll participants in an array of educational and training programs, based on community availability. Again, such services are coordinated with work schedules, with the Case Manager acting as the liaison between the school and the client, monitoring attendance and achievement.

What We Learned

The following is a summary of what we have learned at America Works and suggestions for new workforce policy initiatives.

• People get jobs not so much for what they know, but for whom they know.

Welfare recipients need help finding good jobs. The network of contacts available to others is almost non-existent for the poor. America Works uses a seasoned sales force that strives to assist people by *connecting* them to employment for one simple reason: people get jobs through networks. America Works becomes that network, connecting people to jobs they would not know about or would not have a chance to get, were they to apply for them on their own. Good technical skills, personal presentation and a well-organized resume will only help after a network contact has opened the door. As the adage goes, "It's not what you know, but whom you know" that gets you a job. America Works implements this simple truth by providing job seeking assistance that helps participants identify the necessary contacts to get themselves in the door.

This lesson, simple as it is, has broad ramifications for policies designed to attach disenfranchised people to the labor market. Programs that stress attachment to the labor market are more effective than those that stress technical skills or educational upgrading. Not that education and training are unnecessary, but that they are more helpful when preceded by work. Training seldom has an effect as a first strike in moving people from dependency to independence.

- People lose their jobs not so much for a lack of skills, but for their inability to socially integrate within the work place.

This can be due to cultural differences or outside problems (i.e., an abusive mate, an intrusive welfare bureaucracy). This lesson, again, has profound implications for program policy. Most employment efforts focus on up-front human capital investment. Little is offered once the person gets a job. This would be reversed with intensive on site job support, rapid intervention off the job for problems that might force the person to quit, and minimum initial investment in programs designed to improve the individual. As with the above, get them working and stable, then work on the skills.

- Intervention of a competitive marketplace forces Government to produce.

There is a profound impact on Government by the intervention of free market outcome-driven forces. Bureaucracies are forced to concentrate on measuring outcomes as successful results instead of as service processes. This has occurred already in some of the places America Works is operating. In New York State, since contracting with America Works, the Department of Social Services insists that all its contracts be performance-based. Similarly, in Indianapolis, the child welfare system is going to start using totally performance-based contracting.

The positive impact of this is to ensure that Government is competitive and is a player in the successes and failures of its contractors. Government becomes accountable. In Albany, America Works insists that the county welfare commissioner give referrals to our office and sanction recipients who do not cooperate. If that does not happen we would have trouble meeting our contractual goals for job placement. Linking America Works' success to the local commissioner and holding him accountable assured success for both organizations.

Asay. © 1997 by Creators Syndicate, Inc. Reprinted with permission.

This lesson of learning to create performance driven marketplaces goes beyond making Government accountable. It breaks up the monopoly of process and forces competition between outcome and process-based programs. For America Works it helps welfare departments recognize the foremost goal of getting people off of welfare. It redefines success for an agency.

Empowering Government to compete or join with the private sector in providing services has significant ramifications. In addition to becoming more efficient, as David Osborne documents, it can act as a catalyst for attracting more people to public service. The idea that an entrepreneurial public-minded person could enter Government and not be bound to some of the archaic practices of the past certainly would be appealing to many of those who currently turn away from public service.

• Welfare to work programs fail, in the main, because there is no incentive for them to succeed.

Government-operated programs seldom create incentives to reduce the rolls through job acquisition. Processing paper and protecting the jobs of the bureaucrats prevents a strong work policy from emerging. When contracts are let to private non-profit and profit organizations there are little, if any performance standards strictly based on job finding and retention. Simply, vendors can get most if not all of their money for running a program regardless of how many people get jobs and stick with them.

Of the lessons learned by us at America Works, this is the most important one as we rethink employment policy. The implications for policy would demand no less than a paradigm shift in our thinking and support for interventions that might really work to get people to work.

How to Establish Successful Work Policies

1. Stimulate a competitive marketplace.

This country has been built on private initiatives stimulated and tempered by the public will. When it comes to welfare, it is the public's will organized and operated by government that powers our efforts. However, it is the private marketplace that we expect to absorb people and provide work. Yet business is hardly in the play to increase hiring and reduce the rolls. Inexplicably, the private sector plays a neglected role in welfare to work programs but is expected to do the hiring and to provide all the jobs. The fact is that except for a few specific tax breaks like the Work Opportunity Tax Credit (WOTC), or involvement of low level business people on Workforce Development Boards, the private sector is absent from the debate and the play of welfare policy and, most important, its implementation.

First, we can develop a competitive marketplace to place disenfranchised workers. This is what government does with America Works, but we are tiny and have limited power to effect government policy. Consequently there has been little done by government to build on this competitive model.

The largest employer in this country is Manpower Inc. Its sole purpose is to act as the middleman for companies who need labor and workers capable of being employed. This market developed because of a need by private companies that could not be met internally, and they were willing to pay for it. Central here is the broker function. They get the jobs for people because of who they know. Even for the skilled workers they place, job finding would be difficult. Manpower Inc. facilitates the job finding and match.

Why not establish a similar network for disenfranchised workers? However, in this case, some of the reward or incentive would come from the public sector. Let the government create and administer the incentives offered to vendors only if they succeed in getting people jobs, not for their program's efforts. The government would determine how much it was worth to get an unemployed person working so it receives a reasonable return on its investment. Private entrepreneurs, assessing that the reward is worthy of their initial up front investment, would start ventures. Using this competitiveness model the welfare bureaucracy could be a player as well.

The advantages to this approach are numerous:

• Private capital would flow into an otherwise publicly supported effort.

• Many models would be experimented with. Government would not dictate one-size-fits-all policies.

• Those that place people will continue to do business; those that don't will fold.

• Competition would force efficiencies not encouraged in present day welfare programs.

2. Finance the new marketplace principally through reinvestment of welfare savings.

Fund only those programs that get paid for each person placed and retained in a job. Calculate the savings to the government. Reinvest all or a portion of the savings into new job placement activities. (There is precedent in other program areas to do this at the State level.) Since the payment by Government is made only when the savings have begun to accrue, the investment and return by Government is guaranteed. Entitlement transfer payments are, in effect, used to finance a reduction on dependency.

3. Create a package of tax and other monetary incentives targeted to this new marketplace.

Presently those that exist are directed toward the companies that will finally hire the workers. The fact is, though, most private companies know that with the tax breaks like the WOTC, or a wage subsidy, like those for OJT, come a series of problems. These include hard-to-integrate workers, difficult-to-train employees, and government intrusion. It is why most of these efforts have failed. Placing the incentives squarely into this new sector would encourage the development of programs geared to deal with hard to place workers rather than expecting the permanent employer to take the risk first.

These recommendations require government action. The paradigm shift requires a radical restructuring of the way poor people are given access to the work place. Demonstrations documenting the results of a competitive marketplace for job placement are needed.

"The privatization of welfare services has resulted in . . . poorly run welfare services in the hands of large corporations."

Privatization of Welfare Does Not Benefit Recipients

Bill Berkowitz

As a result of the 1996 welfare reform law, tough federal rules have put pressure on states to reduce their welfare rolls and place recipients in jobs. With the goal of increasing efficiency, many states have chosen to hire private contractors to run segments of their welfare programs, such as skills training and job placement. Bill Berkowitz argues in the following viewpoint that contractors are withholding welfare recipients' access to child care, transportation subsidies, and other services to which they are legally entitled. In addition, these private companies are failing to provide adequate job training or place people in permanent jobs, squandering taxpayer money without public accountability. Berkowitz is an Oakland, California–based writer covering the religious right and related conservative issues.

As you read, consider the following questions:
1. According to the author, what did private companies contend they would accomplish for bloated state and federal welfare bureaucracies?
2. What is an often-voiced complaint about America Works and its job placement practices, as reported by Berkowitz?
3. In the author's opinion, how do the inadequately trained staff at private welfare companies hurt welfare clients?

Excerpted from "Welfare Privatization," by Bill Berkowitz, *Z Magazine*, July/August 2001. Copyright © 2001 by *Z Magazine*. Reprinted with permission.

In 1996, welfare as we knew it was changed radically by the passage and signing of the Personal Responsibility and Work Opportunity Reconciliation Act. The new law gave states unprecedented leeway in determining how the new Temporary Assistance for Needy Families (TANF) and related programs would be handled. Individual states were "liberated," free to set up their own delivery systems within broad federal requirements. Many states, confronted with the daunting task of rapidly implementing this "reform," chose to contract out services to non-profit organizations and for-profit corporations.

Long-time advocates of welfare privatization were delighted. It was difficult to tell which part of the "reform" trifecta made conservatives, and many liberals, happier—the potential multibillion-dollar market; shutting down Aid to Famlies with Dependent Children (AFDC)—the federal government's commitment to a social safety net; or the promise that welfare recipients would no longer get an "easy" ride. . . .

Corporate Ineptitude and Inefficiency

A not so funny thing has happened on the way to a fully privatized welfare system. Many of the largest companies receiving contracts from individual states are facing charges of inefficient, inept, and improper behavior. For almost four years, two of the biggest contractors, Maximus Inc., and Lockheed Martin, have been on a roller coaster ride of limited successes and questionable practices.

Maximus Inc.'s misuse of welfare funds and other rapacious conduct resulted in an early-October 2000 request by Milwaukee-area Democratic Congresspeople Jerry Kleczka and Tom Barrett to the General Accounting Office (GAO) for a full inquiry into practices by private companies hired to manage welfare services. "The increased privatization of state aid programs for the poor has revealed that some for-profit corporations have mishandled welfare funds and contracts," Kleczka said. "Hopefully the GAO can shed some light on just how widespread these problems are and provide Congress with some insight as to how to prevent future misuse and abuse of public funds."

Sandy Felder, Public Sector Coordinator for Service Employees International Union (SEIU), a union representing public employees, told *Covert Action Quarterly* in 1996, "This [welfare reform] is one of the biggest corporate grabs in history." Welfare reform was the most powerful bomb yet to be dropped on America's already shredded social safety net. Mark Dunlea, executive director of the Hunger Action Network of New York, predicted, "The privatization of welfare-related social services . . . will mean a massive handoff from government to the private sector."

"The federal government turned over $16 billion in TANF money to the states without setting any federal standards for privatization," Cecilia Perry, public policy analyst for American Federation of State, County, and Municipal Employees (AFSCME), told me in late December. The early contracts in Wisconsin were particularly egregious in that they were based on setting "perverse incentives aimed at reducing caseloads and making huge profits."

Reducing the Rolls, Eroding Services

Privatization, as touted by its supporters, was to be the guiding hand of welfare reform. It was supposed to convert bloated federal and state bureaucracies into streamlined and cost-effective corporate providers of services. Privatizers held that private companies would also administer welfare regulations more stringently and accurately, deliver more timely and efficient services, and only to the "deserving" poor. At the same time, the private sector would save money for taxpayers. Private companies competing for contracts promised states they would dramatically reduce welfare rolls. Indeed, this is the one area they have been successful. But at what cost, and to whom? . . .

The privatization of welfare services has resulted in numerous examples of the erosion of services. Many programs are seriously under-staffed and there is a woeful lack of public accountability. There are an increasing number of local stories exposing corporate misdeeds under the "cost of doing business"—the amount of money corporations spend to wine, dine, and pay off principals involved in making decisions about awarding contracts. The public gets what it's paying for—poorly run welfare services in the hands of large corporations.

Maximus Inc.

When the 1996 welfare reform bill was signed, it set off a welfare privatization gold rush. . . .

One of the first companies to stake its claim was the McLean, Virginia–based Maximus Inc. *City Limits Weekly* wrote that "Maximus was no stranger to privatization, having been the first company to privatize a welfare system— Los Angeles County's, from 1988 to 1993."

Sharpnack. © 1997 by Joe Sharpnack. Reprinted with permission.

Founded in 1975 by David Mastran, a former Defense Department analyst who worked for the Department of Health, Education, and Welfare during the Nixon administration, Maximus officials were optimistic about the profit potential. Welfare reform "is, as yet, an undetermined revenue pool," company spokesperson Kevin Gedding told the *Los Angeles Times* in 1997. "But there are billions of dollars in potential project work that need to be done in the next four to five years." Bernard Picchi, an analyst of growth stocks for Lehman Brothers, told *Time* the potential market could easily be more than $20 billion a year.

If there is any doubt that welfare "reform" has become a fruitful business, check out these numbers—Maximus has grown from a $50 million operation in 1995 to $105 million in 1996, to $319.5 million in 1999.

Maximus has more than 3,700 employees, located in more than 130 offices across the country. It has recently renewed or signed new contracts in a handful of states including Alaska, Illinois, Tennessee, South Carolina, New Jersey, Kansas, Michigan, Pennsylvania, and Texas. According to the AFSCME *Leader* the company also has operations in Buenos Aires, Argentina and Cairo, Egypt. Maximus has done so well financially that *Forbes* magazine selected it as one of the ten Best Small Companies in America in 1999.

Will the Real Welfare Cheats Stand Up?

Although the bottom line has been soaring, it hasn't been all good news for Maximus. Negative headlines in newspapers around the country have highlighted a series of corporate bad practices including the misappropriation of funds, poor service provision, discriminatory practices at company offices, and financial irregularities. The AFSCME *Leader* found that in 1994, during the pre-welfare "reform" era, "Mississippi froze a child support collection contract with Maximus when costs nearly doubled what the state had spent previously." In West Virginia the company was disqualified from bidding on a state contract "after a state employee was convicted of taking a $20,000 payment from Maximus," which was not charged in the case.

Maximus went public in 1997 and the following year the company came under fire in Connecticut over a $12.8 million contract to run the program providing childcare for working welfare recipients. Within months Maximus found its operations in disarray. *Time* reported, "More than half of the 17,000 bills submitted by child-care providers were over 30 days late in being paid." Day-care centers were confronted with decisions about turning away children and parents trying to contact the company found that the telephone system had virtually collapsed. "In terms of service here, they've been abysmal," noted Rick Melita, a spokesperson for the Connecticut State Employees Association. "They underbid, over-promised, and they didn't deliver," he told *Ethnic NewsWatch*.

More "Glaring Mistakes"

The breakdown in Connecticut was a harbinger of things to come. Significant complaints against Maximus surfaced in other states as well. Privatization advocates have long considered Wisconsin, where Maximus provides a complete spectrum of Wisconsin Works (W-2) programs, the showplace of welfare "reform." Since 1997, Maximus garnered more than $100 million in contracts in Milwaukee for welfare related services. During the past several months, the *Milwaukee Journal Sentinel* has reported on growing dissatisfaction with and rampant improprieties in the way Maximus is running its contracts. A coalition of Milwaukee-area church groups, representing 50 churches in the city and suburbs, and 6 state lawmakers, including supporters of "welfare reform," have called for the termination of a $46 million Maximus contract that provides job training and other services to welfare recipients.

The *Milwaukee Journal Sentinel* cited a late-July 2000 audit by the Legislative Audit Bureau that "found nearly $800,000 in questionable spending by Maximus." This included "thousands in W-2 funds spent on soliciting contracts in other states, concerts for W-2 clients by Broadway singer Melba Moore and a holiday party for Maximus employees." Jennifer Reinert, who heads the state agency that oversees W-2, said auditors found no evidence of fraud, and she blamed the problems on "sloppy bookkeeping." Maximus has agreed to pay back $500,000 for "improper spending of taxpayer W-2 money," and to spend another $500,000 on "extra services for the poor in Milwaukee County to try to make amends."

Milwaukee Journal Sentinel columnist Eugene Kane wondered how "a large sophisticated company like Maximus—with welfare reform contracts in more than two dozen states—could have made so many glaring mistakes." Maximus, "one of five agencies hired to help create a welfare 'reform' system here that ended up being so confusing and poorly run that in little more than three years, loads of frustrated poor people opted out of the system. Cutting poor families off the dole proved so successful, W-2 enjoyed a huge surplus of funds, mainly because the program was drastically overbudgeted in the first place.". . .

Lockheed Martin

Lockheed Martin is probably the biggest and most well known company involved in welfare privatization. In the *Nation*, William D. Hartung and Jennifer Washburn describe how America's largest weapons manufacturer designed a division of the company—Lockheed Martin Information Management Services (IMS)—"to run full-scale welfare programs in Texas and Arizona." Coming on the heels of the company's $885 million Pentagon contract, Lockheed Martin's grand strategy includes allowing private companies "to run entire government programs; in the case of welfare and Medicaid, moreover, these are essential services, affecting the most disenfranchised members of the population, who are least able to defend their rights."

Questionable Business Practices

Lockheed Martin's controversial and checkered history makes Maximus Inc. look like a Girl Scout troop. Hartung and Washburn: "This is, after all, one of the companies whose fondness for doling out bribes moved Congress to pass the Foreign Corrupt Practices Act in 1977; the company whose multibillion dollar overcharges on the C-54 transport plane made 'cost overrun' a household phrase; and the company whose 1971 government bailout—a $250 million loan guarantee with no strings attached—inspired former Senator William Proxmire to coin the phrase 'corporate welfare.'" Of course, there's the legendary $600 toilet seat Lockheed produced for the Navy. . . .

Lockheed Martin's [1995] bid to completely overhaul Texas's welfare system was rejected. However, the company received several major contracts. It has been quick to take credit for finding jobs for thousands of Texans who had been receiving welfare. As it is with many other states, it's difficult to measure the long-term effects of Lockheed's programs since, as Miriam Rosen reports in the *Dallas Observer*, the state legislature doesn't track them. Rosen says, "the chief concern of many frontline poverty workers . . . is the lack of research on the consequences of welfare reform. No one knows whether Lockheed Martin's success stories will end up back on the dole in a few years."

Kim Olsen, an organizer at the Association of Community Organizations for Reform Now (ACORN), told Rosen she had informally interviewed some 700 welfare recipients since the reforms took effect. Olsen "believes that Lockheed Martin's tactics have left many aid recipients in the dark about benefits for which they are eligible—including educational and child-care subsidies."

Lockheed has won more than two dozen contracts providing several states with case management, skills training, and job placement assistance. However, its reputation as a service provider has come under criticism. In Baltimore, Maryland, for example, where the company won a three-year contract to collect child support, Lockheed "failed to meet performance goals" in its first year. In California, the company and the state "mutually agreed to cancel a contract for Lockheed Martin to build a computerized tracking system for collecting child support . . . [when] the system's projected costs had skyrocketed—from $99 million to $277 million."

America Works . . . but Does It Really?

Founded in 1984 as a private for-profit company by Peter Cove and Lee Bowes, America Works has become another company eagerly sharing in the privatization of welfare boom, with contracts in New York City, Albany, Baltimore, Indianapolis, and Miami. According to its website, its mission is to "change people's lives by lifting them from welfare dependency into the productive world of employment."

The company's founders believe that poor work habits are major obstacles to the long-term unemployed. Attaining and keeping jobs requires knowing how to be "on time and reliable, take direction and behave appropriately." It is this "tough love" approach or "boot-camp-style job readiness" welfare-to-work services that has made America Works the darling of Mayor Rudolph Giuliani (NY), who made cutting the welfare rolls the centerpiece of his Administration. Giuliani "raised some eyebrows a year ago," according to the *New York Times'* Jason DeParle, by bringing the above-mentioned Jason Turner, "one of the nation's most uncompromising critics of public assistance," on board to run the city's welfare agency. "Turner, a veteran of Wisconsin's anti-welfare campaign, designed his first welfare plan in junior high school, and he has been refining his craft ever since." America Works' approach has also received considerable positive coverage in the mainstream media.

Disregarding Tough Cases

The Hunger Action Network's Mark Dunlea says that the company "focuses on finding entry-level positions such as receptionists, secretary, mail-room clerk, word processor, cashier, security or warehouse worker . . . [with] a typical annual salary . . . rang[ing] from $15,500 to $18,000." An often-voiced criticism about America Works is that it skims off the best potential clients and disregards the hard-core cases. "For example," says Dunlea, "a worker who has a family emergency and fails to comply with an attendance policy— far stricter than in most workplaces—is typically kicked out of the program."

A 1996 audit by New York State Comptroller H. Carl McCall pointed out that America Works was under contract with the state to place AFDC recipients in private sector, unsubsidized jobs. The company was paid by the state when a client either: "(a) enrolled in the program, or (b) was placed in a job by the program, or (c) retained the job for at least 90 days." Dunlea cites an AFSCME report claiming that America Works has received more than $1 million from New York State "for people who never found jobs and for placements that never became permanent.". . .

Privatization's False Promises

Privatization as the engine powering welfare reform was supposed to replace federal and state bureaucracies with streamlined, cost-effective corporate service providers. Privatizers believed that private companies would administer welfare regulations more stringently and accurately, deliver services more efficiently, and focus on only those who really deserved benefits. Saving the taxpayers money was another appealing promise. Companies competing for contracts assured states that they would dramatically reduce the welfare rolls.

Has the privatization of welfare delivered on its promises? Have private companies and enterprising nonprofits transformed the old welfare system with the outcome of long-term employment with decent pay for former welfare recipients? Max Sawicky, economist at the Washington, DC–based Economic Policy Institute, is troubled by the fact that the so-called "success [of welfare privatization] was announced before the results are in."

In a 1997 speech, Lawrence W. Reed, President of the conservative Midland, Michigan–based Mackinac Center for Public Policy, touted privatization as the wave of the future: "The superiority of [privatization] . . . is now approaching the status of undisputed, conventional wisdom: the private sector exacts a toll from the inefficient for their poor performance, compels the service provider or asset owner to concern himself with the wishes of customers, and spurs a dynamic, never-ending pursuit of excellence—all without any of the political baggage that haunts the public sector as elements of its very nature."

Rolling in the Profits

After four years of welfare reform there is evidence that privatization has been successful, not for the people who were supposed to be moved out of poverty, but for corporate profiteers.

• While welfare privatization has delivered drastic reductions in caseloads and welfare rolls, it has not moved recipients from the "underclass" to the working class. Privatization is not efficiently delivering job training and support services to those who need them.

• The financial bonuses privatizers receive for reducing caseloads create an incentive to terminate clients' benefits, not to assist them in climbing out of poverty.

• As in the case of Curtis and Associates, staff working for private companies often have neither the credentials nor the training to handle their caseloads. Consequently, clients do not receive services they need, and to which they are entitled, such as childcare, transportation subsidies, and medical care.

• As Wisconsin, New York, and Texas have learned to their chagrin, companies like Maximus and Lockheed Martin blithely spend public money from other jurisdictions to wine, dine, and pay off decision-makers in the pursuit of new contracts.

• The states and local governments that contract with corporations for welfare services have not instituted any form of systematic oversight.

• Because information about large private contractors is not centralized, it is not unusual for a company in hot water one place to pick up new contracts at the same time in another state—or in another county in the same state.

• Ultimately, for-profit corporations are accountable to their shareholders, not to the communities they are hired to serve.

Spurred by revelations of Maximus's questionable activities, Milwaukee-area Democratic Congresspeople Jerry Kleczka and Tom Barrett are hoping the federal General Accounting Office will fully investigate the practices of private companies hired to manage welfare services. As we move closer to welfare reauthorization, the GAO needs to vigorously take on the Congresspeople's request. In the meantime, corporations will continue prospecting for gold among the poor.

Periodical Bibliography

The following articles have been selected to supplement the diverse views presented in this chapter.

Paul Clark — "Governors Are the Real Welfare Kings," *Wanderer*, October 14, 1999.

Jason DeParle — "A Welfare Plan Justifies Hopes and Some Fear," *New York Times*, January 15, 1999.

Jason DeParle — "Wisconsin Welfare Experiment: Easy to Say, Not So Easy to Do," *New York Times*, October 18, 1998.

Catherine Edwards — "The Truth About Charitable Choice," *Insight on the News*, March 26, 2001.

Larry Elder — "Daring to Question the Welfare State," *Human Events*, July 16, 2001.

Alan Finder — "Some Private Efforts See Success in Job Hunt for Those on Welfare," *New York Times*, June 16, 1998.

Albert R. Hunt — "Faith-Based Efforts: The Promise and Limitations," *Wall Street Journal*, August 12, 1999.

Star Parker — "Eliminating Government Welfare in the Next Millennium: How Do We Take Care of This Nation's Most Needy?" Coalition on Urban Renewal and Education, 2001. www.urbancure.org.

James L. Payne — "Welfare 'Cuts'?" *American Enterprise*, November/December 1997.

Andrew C. Revkin — "Welfare Policies Alter the Face of Food Lines," *New York Times*, February 26, 1999.

Amy L. Sherman — "Navigating Charitable Choice," *Christian Century*, July 5, 2000.

Robert A. Sirico — "Restoring Charity: Ethical Principles for a New Welfare Policy," Acton Institute, 2001. www.acton.org.

Michael Tanner — "Corrupting Charity: Why Government Should Not Fund Faith-Based Charities," *Cato Institute Briefing Papers*, March 22, 2001. www.cato.org.

Jessica Yates — "Privatization and Welfare Reform," *Welfare Information Network Issue Notes*, February 1997. www.welfareinfo.org.

CHAPTER 4

How Should Welfare Be Reformed?

Chapter Preface

By the time President Bill Clinton completed his first year in office in 1994, the number of families receiving assistance under the welfare program known as Aid to Families with Dependent Children (AFDC) had reached an all-time high of 5 million. Such a large number of recipients bolstered the claims of welfare's critics, who warned that once young mothers were on welfare, there were few incentives for them to leave, since the package of benefits often surpassed what could be earned through work in the private sector. With many Democrats and Republicans alike coming to share this view of welfare as causing dependency, welfare reform moved to the forefront of political debate.

The 1994 congressional elections gave Republicans control of Congress and strong support for their "Contract with America" platform of conservative reforms, which included a plan for welfare reform called the "personal responsibility act," according to Michael Tanner, a researcher at the Cato Institute, a libertarian think tank. The Republicans' first version of welfare reform was vetoed by President Bill Clinton, but in August 1996, Congress passed and Clinton signed a compromise bill known as the Personal Responsibility and Work Opportunity Reconciliation Act (PRAWORA).

PRAWORA's changes to the welfare program were designed to encourage work while reducing dependency and out-of-wedlock childbearing. First and foremost, the law ended the entitlement to benefits: Single mothers and their children would be subject to federal time limits on benefits and work requirements. The law replaced AFDC with a program called Temporary Assistance for Needy Families (TANF), which limits recipients to two years of welfare benefits after which they must find work or their benefits will be reduced or terminated. Families are limited to a lifetime total of five years of welfare benefits. The TANF program's funds are part of a block grant, meaning that states have the freedom to administer their welfare programs as long as they comply with the federal time limits and work requirements. The law addresses out-of-wedlock childbearing by requiring unmarried teenage mothers to live at home and stay in school in order to receive money. In addition, states can deny additional benefits to women on welfare who bear more children.

The law continues to generate debate. Supporters of PRAWORA point out that as welfare recipients are forced to find work or risk losing their benefits, able-bodied recipients increasingly have opted to reenter the workforce. Says Michael W. Lynch of the Reason Institute, a libertarian think tank, "By removing the barriers to work—in many cases, simply taking away people's excuses—[welfare administrators] . . . have put people . . . to work." According to this view, past expectations of welfare recipients have been too low, and acknowledging that they are capable of fending for themselves in the working world has benefited them.

Many opponents of PRAWORA argue that the new law has increased the ranks of the working poor and makes unrealistic demands of poor single mothers. Notes *Business Week* magazine, "The recent data show that while millions of former welfare mothers have jobs, their incomes are often lower than before the reforms were enacted. . . . Even those experts who point to the more encouraging studies agree that a substantial number of former welfare moms are floundering."

Most observers agree that PRAWORA has significantly reduced the welfare rolls. According to the Council of State Governments, by June 1999, fifteen states had welfare roll declines of over 60 percent, and overall, welfare rolls had fallen 49 percent from their high of 5 million families in the early 1990s. What is not clear is whether former welfare recipients are moving out of poverty and into stable, self-supporting lives. How the welfare system can best be reformed to achieve a genuine reduction in poverty is debated and discussed by the authors in the following chapter.

"[Reducing the welfare rolls] will require a moral resolve about why welfare dependency is bad."

The Government Should Discourage Welfare Dependency

Charles Murray

In the following viewpoint, Charles Murray asserts that in order to encourage welfare mothers to change their behavior and join the workforce, government must ensure that remaining on public assistance offers a lower standard of living than low-wage work does. Although politicians talked tough about ending the entitlement to welfare during the passage of the 1996 welfare reform bill, the pressure on recipients to get jobs has eased, and people are finding loopholes in the complex welfare laws. For the increasingly unmotivated and unreceptive clients still on the rolls, welfare remains a comfortable alternative to employment. According to Murray, if government does not back up its tough message with more punitive reforms, dependency will continue and the welfare rolls will increase again. Murray is the Bradley Fellow at the American Enterprise Institute, a conservative think tank.

As you read, consider the following questions:
1. What is the "first" reality behind the plunging welfare rolls, according to the author?
2. How did the Victorians achieve success in helping the poor, according to Murray?

Excerpted from "What Government Must Do: Make Welfare Unappealing or Reform Will Fail," by Charles Murray, *American Enterprise*, January/February 1998. Copyright © 1998 by American Enterprise Institute. Reprinted with permission.

Years ago I worked for a research company that evaluated social programs for the federal government. One time I was heading a team assessing a program for troubled inner-city teenagers. As the evaluation approached its end, no quantitative measure showed the program had accomplished anything. I gave the draft of the report to the program's staff.

They were unhappy and angry. Maybe what they'd accomplished didn't show up in the numbers, they said, but dammit, they dealt in human lives, not numbers, and they knew they'd had an impact. I can't change the numbers, I replied, but we'll go through your files, pull out the ones that represent your biggest successes, and I'll write them up as case histories of what the program can accomplish at its best.

So we went through the files together. And we couldn't find any successes. The staff had been thinking about Sally, let's call her, who in the first year of the program had come back to school, pulled her grades up, and stayed away from drugs. But when we looked up what had happened to Sally since she'd left the program, it turned out she had dropped out of school and was back on drugs. It wasn't that our numbers had failed to capture important outcomes, but that the staff hadn't checked up on their success stories for a while, and they had regressed to where they started. In the end, I had to make what I could from a few examples of fragmentary progress.

Returning to Hard Realities

This history is a cautionary tale for thinking about what we can expect from welfare devolution. In [their writings on welfare reform, the journalists] Aaron Steelman and Amy Sherman tell an entirely believable account of how hard it is even for the most well-meaning and dedicated people to change people's lives, and we must ask even of this scattered good news how many of the success stories will still be successes a year from now. It is time to return to a few hard realities that have been slipping from sight as we become accustomed to news about plunging welfare rolls.

The first reality is that welfare rolls have not gone down because of actual changes in law or the operation of welfare bureaucracies. As recent studies reveal, the rolls have been dropping at about the same rate before and after the provisions of any given welfare reform have gone into effect. What changed, if not the laws? Don't rely on the growing economy for explanations. Look at the welfare rolls in the economic expansions of the 1960s and 1980s: In the Reagan years, welfare rolls remained steady; during the Johnson boom years, when unemployment stood at less than 4 percent, the welfare rolls soared. The growing economy of the 1990s increased the ability of welfare recipients to get jobs if they wanted them, but the trigger for the change in wanting jobs must be sought somewhere besides growth in gross national product (GNP).

More Government Programs Will Not End Poverty

Liberals have belatedly come to the realization that something is wrong with the welfare system. They are now willing to see the program "reformed." However, they remain captives of the idea that there is a programmatic response to poverty. Most liberal proposals for welfare reform involve additional government spending and new government programs—for job training, child care, education, and many other initiatives.

That approach seems to reflect a stubborn refusal to learn from past results. Nearly all such programmatic responses have been tried before—and failed miserably. For example, more than 150 job-training programs have failed to move large numbers of welfare recipients into the job market. Is there any reason—except blind faith in government—to believe that another one will work?

Liberals must understand that solving the problem of poverty is beyond the power of government programs. Liberal approaches to fighting poverty have the best of intentions. But they have been tried before and have almost inevitably made the situation worse. The next question is whether conservative reforms are any better.

Michael Tanner, *The End of Welfare*, 1996.

In seeking that trigger, we know this much for sure: For a few years, the politicians, including [then] President Clinton, talked very tough indeed. Two years and out. No more entitlement to welfare. Get a job or you're going to find yourself on the streets. Legislation began to pass in individual states, then in Washington. The media gave headline coverage to the direst predictions—the coming of Calcutta on the Hudson, a million children thrown into poverty, etc. The word spread to the street. The least attentive welfare recipient could not avoid being bombarded with messages that her world was about to come crashing down.

My interpretation of the trends in welfare rolls is that the rhetoric worked. The welfare population includes a fairly large number of women who could work if they wanted to badly enough, and all the hoopla moved some proportion of those women to act. This is not a trivial accomplishment. But neither is it necessarily going to continue. Once we look beyond that top layer of competent and readily motivated women, we find another hard reality: The interventions of outsiders—whether they be government social workers or church volunteers or socially conscious employers—require a receptive client. Receptive means first that she is not already deeply habituated to the life she lives. Receptive also means the client knows she is in dire trouble unless she gets her life in order. Absent either of those conditions, social interventions end up with evaluations concluding that the intervention had no statistical effect.

Help the Deserving First

I write these pessimistic cautions as someone who believes that only the private realm of employers, philanthropy, churches, and neighbors can succeed in reducing the size of the underclass. In many ways, Sherman and Steelman are describing a resurrection of the model I admire most: the extensive and energetic social philanthropy developed in late-nineteenth-century England by the Victorians, a private system that enjoyed enormous success in propagating middle-class virtues down to the lowest ranks of the British working class. But while Sherman's and Steelman's heroes are heading in the right direction, they face a problem: Neither of the conditions for a receptive clientele applies broadly today.

Consider the first condition for receptivity, that the client not be deeply habituated to the life she lives. Of those left on the rolls, many are so alienated from regular schedules, work habits, and responsible behavior that no one knows how to make them into good workers. If helping agencies of any kind are to be effective, they must perform triage. In language the Victorians would have used, they must not shrink from distinguishing between the deserving and undeserving poor.

This doesn't mean the undeserving must be abandoned. The Victorians accepted that they could feed and clothe them. But the Victorians focused their most energetic efforts on the deserving. America's helping agencies, public and private, have yet to accept that (1) from an ethical standpoint we should first help those who are trying to help themselves, and (2) from a practical standpoint they are just about the only ones we can help. A church shouldn't be putting its limited resources into helping young women who have to be pushed and cajoled to look for a job. It should be helping young women who have lined up a job but can't find a ride to work. A company shouldn't reserve job slots for employees who must be treated with kid gloves lest they get in a fight with their supervisors; it should be on the lookout for those whose job records may be bad but are saying, "Just give me a chance, and you can fire me the first time I'm five minutes late." Help those who are receptive to help, *let it be openly seen that those who are receptive to help receive preferential treatment*, and you will have begun the process whereby more and more people become receptive.

Slipping Through Loopholes, Losing Motivation to Change

The second condition of receptivity, urgent motivation to change, is also weak. Even if it is true that today's private helpers need a dose of good old-fashioned judgmentalism, most of the blame for the difficulties they face falls on the government. The Victorians had the crucial advantage of working alongside a government that believed in the rule of "less eligibility," meaning that public assistance had to provide a standard of living less desirable (less eligible) than that enjoyed by the lowest-paid worker. The Victorians worked in an environment in which to have a baby without help from the baby's father or one's own parents was to be forced to rely on the kindness of strangers. Thus did the Victorians find a clientele motivated by the prospect of hovering disaster, and thus did they achieve great things.

In contrast, today's employers and church committees are finding that whatever momentary scare they had working for them is rapidly dissipating. The Clinton White House, with the collaboration of a Republican Congress, . . . [gutted] the tough aspects of the original welfare reform bill. Social workers, many of whom were hostile toward the welfare reform bill in the first place, are looking for excuses to relax the pressure to get jobs. Ways are being found, as they are always found with complex welfare systems, to slip through loopholes. These changes are known to the clientele—the street-level awareness of changes in atmosphere at the welfare office is as keen as Wall Street's sensitivity to changes in atmosphere at the Federal Reserve.

Get the Ground Rules Right

Women are already seeing through the propaganda. The welfare system still provides a better living than a low-wage job, it is still a more reliable source of money than the boyfriend, and if you know the ins and outs you can stay on it indefinitely. For the last few years, those who were trying to help move welfare women to work were dealing with women who were genuinely worried about what the future held. That is decreasingly true. Before the private helpers can do good, the government has to get the ground rules right. The government moved in that direction in 1996 but then lost its nerve.

My gloomy prediction? Faced with a difficult job at best, and trying to deal with an increasingly unreceptive clientele, churches and employers and local groups will have fewer and fewer successes to show for their efforts. The welfare rolls will start to move up again, and the pundits will say it proves that the private sector can't do the job after all. This can be avoided. But it will require a moral resolve about why welfare dependency is bad, why illegitimacy is bad, and why they must be reduced, that the President never had and that Congress has lost.

"Welfare reform has not fundamentally improved the living standards of many of the families it has affected."

Welfare Recipients Need More Government Assistance

Jared Bernstein and Mark Greenberg

Jared Bernstein and Mark Greenberg contend in the following viewpoint that government should do more to ensure the economic well-being of working families who have left the welfare rolls since the passage of the 1996 welfare reform law. According to the authors, many former welfare recipients are struggling to make ends meet, and families who remain on the welfare rolls are faced with losing their assistance under federally imposed time limits. As the welfare law comes up for congressional reauthorization in 2002, the authors assert that low-income working families should have expanded access to food stamps, health care, and child care, and that welfare recipients unable to find employment should be granted more flexible time limits. Jared Bernstein is an economist at the Economic Policy Institute, a nonpartisan think tank. Mark Greenberg is a senior staff attorney at the Center for Law and Social Policy, a nonprofit organization conducting research on law and policy affecting the poor.

As you read, consider the following questions:
1. In the authors' opinion, what is the true goal of welfare reform?
2. What is the best way to improve the welfare law as it comes up for reauthorization, according to the authors?

In 2002 Congress will revisit Temporary Assistance for Needy Families (TANF), often known as welfare reform. Many progressives, ourselves included, fought hard against the program that passed in 1996. We judged it too punitive and too far from the spirit of progressive reform, which would have focused less on reducing caseloads and more on both promoting employment and improving the well-being of low-income families with children. We worried that the low-wage labor market, which had been deteriorating for decades, provided little opportunity for families forced to leave public assistance. We feared that without work supports, such as child care and expanded earnings subsidies, the economic circumstances of some of our most vulnerable families would be severely diminished. We argued that the block grant funding approach of the new program revoked the important counter-cyclical feature of the entitlement program that TANF replaced.

Focusing on the Goal of True Reform

So far, the evidence reveals that many of our fears have not been borne out, at least not to the extent we predicted. The labor market, particularly the low-wage sector, improved in ways we never foresaw. This in turn led to the first persistent real-wage gains experienced there in two-and-a-half decades. These wage gains, the new welfare policy, and other pro-work policies have attracted more low-income single mothers into paid employment. Some states, albeit too few, made considerable efforts to smooth the path to the labor market by providing the needed work supports to both the poor and near poor. And, thankfully, there has as yet been no recession.

Yet while many of our fears have not been realized, it remains the case that TANF has not focused enough on the goal of true reform: the improvement of the economic well-being of poor families with children. Caseloads have fallen sharply and employment rates have soared, but welfare reform has not fundamentally improved the living standards of many of the families it has affected. And if that's the case in this, the best economy in 30 years, what can we expect in a downturn?

At the heart of the TANF reauthorization debate is an assessment of the relative roles of welfare reform itself and the strong economy. This is crucial if we are to avoid over- or undercrediting the policy change. We also believe this debate should not stop at the gates of welfare reform, but should address the larger question of how to lift the living standards of all working families, particularly those who have only recently benefited from the boom. These families have long responded to the personal responsibility clauses enshrined in the law that created TANF, yet their good-faith efforts are inadequately reciprocated by public obligation. So the reauthorization debate represents a historical opportunity to frame a set of policies outside of the welfare system designed to end working poverty as we know it.

Certainly, the 107th Congress may not be very receptive to a progressive set of reforms, especially since many will be arguing that the program has been an unqualified success. Yet . . . this is a fine time to introduce a progressive agenda built around work. The core idea is that those who make a good-faith contribution to the nation's economy should never live in privation. They and their children should see their living standards rise over time, and if the market fails to deliver that result, then there is an explicit role for public policy to do so.

What Welfare Reform Did

Known as the Personal Responsibility and Work Opportunity Reconciliation Act of 1996 (PRWORA), the controversial law included far more than welfare reform. Much of it was simply designed to cut benefits or spending in low-income programs. For example, the law sharply limited the situations in which legal immigrants can qualify for public benefits, narrowed the circumstances in which children qualify for disability benefits, and imposed an array of large and small reductions in the Food Stamp Program.

The centerpiece, though, was repeal of the Aid to Families with Dependent Children (AFDC) program, and the enactment of a system of block grants to states—Temporary Assistance for Needy Families (TANF). In the block grant structure, states qualify each year for a lump sum of federal money, with most states' allocations basically frozen at 1994 or 1995 federal funding levels through 2002. With their block grants, states were expected to run time-limited, work-oriented programs of cash assistance for poor families. The law eliminated federal entitlements: No family has a federal right to assistance, and states have no obligation whatsoever to provide families with welfare benefits. States cannot use federal funds to assist families for more than 60 months (subject to limited exceptions) but are free to provide assistance for shorter periods. States can use their block grant funds to help families prepare for, find, and keep jobs, but states are not required to do so and can use their block grant funds for a wide array of purposes. The law created a strong incentive to cut welfare caseloads—because there was no duty to assist families, states knew that they would get the same amount of funds whether their caseloads went up or down, and the surest way to avoid federal penalties was to bring down the state's caseload.

"WELL THEN, YOU'LL JUST HAVE TO TIGHTEN YOUR BELTS A LITTLE *MORE*...."

Borgman. © 1996 by Cincinnati Enquirer. Reprinted with permission.

What was Congress trying to achieve? Different people had different goals, and the law reflects these differing views. For some the 1996 law was largely about cutting welfare caseloads or reducing spending; for some it was about promoting work; for some it was about broadening state flexibility, reducing federal authority, and curtailing individual rights; and for some it was about reducing out-of-wedlock births. For much of the public, though, the goal was that people who were able to work should do so. . . .

Personal Responsibility and Public Obligation

TANF reauthorization may represent the best opportunity in the next congressional session to articulate progressive values and visions about welfare policy. To be sure, the balance of power at the federal level will limit the potential for progressive change. But we believe that what's occurred thus far can be framed in a way that builds on welfare reform's more positive aspects. Moreover, to work solely within the confines of a welfare program, however progressive, is to miss a historic opportunity to expand our vision of reform to include improvement of the social welfare of all families, not simply those leaving the welfare rolls.

Increasing Public Obligation

The starting premise is that if the polity wants to promote work and improve the well-being of families with children, personal responsibility must be accompanied by public obligation. As the evidence has shown, most former welfare families have embraced the "PR"—the personal responsibility—in PRWORA (indeed, many had always embraced it). Millions more low-income working families never joined the welfare rolls. These families are playing by the rules; yet even in the best economy in decades, they need more help. For others personal responsibility by itself will never lead to sustained employment without help from government. The best use of reauthorization would be to build on and expand the positive aspects of welfare reform—policies designed to ensure the economic well-being of working families—and to restructure those components of the current law that work against this goal. We also need to remember that a recession may be lurking out there somewhere, and that the legislation, as it stands, is unprepared for this looming possibility.

The reauthorization agenda should include at least these six points.

1. *Change the law's central focus from reducing caseloads to reducing poverty.* In 1996 Congress emphasized the need to cut welfare caseloads and states responded impressively. But can states respond equally well to a national goal of reducing, and ultimately eliminating, child and family poverty? Block grant funds alone are not enough to accomplish this goal. Yet states should be required to explain how they will use block grant funds and other state resources to fight poverty, and they should be measured by their success in doing so. This does not mean a shift away from trying to promote employment: The most straightforward way to reduce family poverty today is to help parents enter the labor force, maintain employment, and gain access to the supports that are supposed to be available to working families.

2. *Increase funding and make states more accountable for how they use their funds.* If states are being asked to broaden their focus from reducing welfare to addressing poverty, then they will need more resources, even if their welfare caseloads have shrunk. There should be continuing efforts to enhance the funding in states that receive the least resources in relation to their population of low-income families. At the same time, states should describe how they plan to use block grant funds, report on how they actually used them, and make a commitment that funds will not be diverted to refinance other parts of the state budget.

3. *Expand and improve the supports for low-income working families.* The availability of child care and health care assistance needs to be increased, and there should be a major effort to simplify and improve the accessibility of food stamps, Medicaid, and other benefits that could improve the well-being of families headed by parents in low-wage jobs.

4. *Revisit the federal time limit.* In most states, the families remaining on the welfare rolls haven't reached their time limits yet, but they soon will. There is no good reason to cut off help to families in which the parents cannot find steady work or earn enough to support a family. At minimum, time limit rules should be revised to allow more flexibility. States should be allowed to stop the clock for working families while continuing to provide assistance. States should also be able to provide extensions to working families and families in which

a parent cannot find or maintain work. And states should be encouraged to operate publicly funded jobs programs instead of terminating assistance for families who are able to do some work but unable to maintain unsubsidized employment.

5. *Eliminate the federal bias against education and training efforts.* At the very least, it should be up to each state to decide what role education and training will play in its welfare efforts. Federal law could go further and require states to explain how they will use block grant funds to expand access to education and training programs for low-income families and how they will effectively coordinate their welfare reform efforts with broader state strategies for work force development.

6. *Build in economic stabilizers.* The strong economy and, in particular, the tight labor market have been central to TANF's functioning thus far. In the absence of full employment, work-based welfare reform will be severely challenged unless it ceases to depend solely on private-sector employment opportunities. The current law has a "contingency fund" intended to make additional resources available to states during an economic downturn; but as a practical matter, the fund is structured in a way that will be of little or no use to all or most states. A true contingency plan for a recession (or even for a weaker labor market) would involve providing states access to additional funding during an economic downturn and encouraging them to provide both assistance and, when needed, publicly funded employment if private-sector employment is unavailable.

Beyond TANF

The larger goal of public policy should be a transformation of the low-wage labor market and the economic prospects of the working poor. Historically, working families have been forced to turn to welfare for two reasons: first, because other systems—such as child support, unemployment compensation, the disability benefits system, and parental leave—failed or were not available; and second, because the compensation available to working parents in the low-wage labor market was insufficient to meet their families' basic needs. The next stage of welfare reform provides an opportunity to foster a broader discussion of policies that can promote work and support families. We have in mind a four-legged policy stool.

1. *Maintain full employment.* Throughout this piece, we've noted the importance of tight labor markets. Maintaining full employment is still the most effective social policy in terms of lifting the economic prospects of poor working families. Much of what we strive for pales by comparison. Yet too often progressives have treated full employment as a happy accident—as something that's outside our purview.

The reversal of two decades of declining earnings among low-wage workers was largely a function of achieving full employment in the latter 1990s. This was no accident of fate. It stemmed largely from the actions of the Federal Reserve; the Fed's liberalized interest rate policy allowed the unemployment rate to fall below the level that most economists had argued would trigger runaway inflation. True, other factors were at play, including a strong dollar holding down import prices and a surge in productivity growth, but other factors are always at play. It now looks as if the old speed-limit rules were not only wrong; they consigned millions of poor working families to falling real wages and incomes during the 1980s and early 1990s. We must use the reauthorization debate to enshrine full employment as our most sacred social policy.

2. *Raise pretax wages.* The minimum wage needs to be set high enough to create a reasonable floor on the low-wage labor market. Given the limited bargaining power of low-wage workers (only about 5 percent belong to unions), the minimum wage is a crucial labor market institution protecting the lowest-paid workers—who are disproportionately minorities and females—from exploitation. . . .

Our research suggests that the minimum could at least be set back to its 1979 peak of $6.75 in today's dollars without generating job losses. . . .

3. *Raise after-tax earnings.* Here the best policy by far is the Earned Income Tax Credit (EITC). It is politically popular, its antipoverty effects are well established, and it is very finely targeted at poor working families. Some problems with the EITC have recently been identified, such as the marriage penalty and the high marginal tax rate faced by those who are on the downslope of the program. But excellent plans are

afoot to repair these, expand the policy, and lift the incomes of the working poor and near-poor higher still. . . . Also, 15 states have introduced add-on earned-income tax credits, thus allowing families that receive the federal credit to collect an additional, smaller benefit from the state. (In only 10 of these cases are the credits refundable, so the benefit is unlikely to reach most of the working poor in the other five states.). . .

4. *Support work.* Regardless of a person's income, work-related expenses can be very significant. Research shows that for low-income families the costs of working can easily absorb 30 percent of family income. Given the pay scales in the low-wage labor market, the instability of employment there (which is itself related to the lack of work supports), and the lack of fringe benefits such as paid sick days or maternity leave, low-wage workers cannot meet their basic needs without help. Perhaps the most obvious barrier to steady employment for these families is child care. Transportation assistance has also proved useful, particularly in solving spatial mismatch problems in areas where the laborers can't get to the jobs. Health insurance is another obvious problem for the working poor. . . .

Reviewing TANF's Impact on Poor Families

The last few years have witnessed some truly amazing changes in social and economic policy. A Democratic president signed a largely Republican bill that ended the entitlement of welfare and emphasized work more than any past reform effort had done. At the same time, economic conditions in the low-wage labor market improved far more than we could ever have expected.

The overlap of these two events has led to greatly reduced welfare caseloads and a lot more single mothers working in the paid labor market. That much is known. But as TANF comes up for reauthorization in 2002, a much more fundamental question must be addressed: Has welfare reform improved the well-being of poor families with children?

Our review of the evidence suggests that for some it has but for many it has not. There's more work but not much more disposable income, especially after one takes into account the expenses associated with work. For the families who haven't been able to break into the labor market, the tattered safety net is providing less help than ever. Furthermore, the TANF program, which has been greatly supported by the strong economy, is not prepared for the next recession, which seems to be edging closer by the quarter.

Yet it would be a mistake to write welfare reform off as a failure. The evidence does not support such a judgment. Some states put their surplus welfare dollars to good use, paving the way into the labor market with earnings subsidies and work supports. These programs in tandem with the tight labor market provided employment opportunities that seem to have made a real difference in the lives of former welfare recipients, many of whom report that they are happier with their lives now that they are off public assistance. It appears that these families have a sense of hope for the future that was absent in the past.

Reducing Punitive Aspects, Making Work Pay

The reauthorization debate should be used to keep that hope alive and to extend it to all low-income families. To do so means fixing the program from within by strengthening the positive aspects of the welfare-to-work approach and giving states the resources and responsibility to make work pay and to sustain the gains made so far even through the next recession. It means softening some of the punitive aspects of the program that have been shown to cause unnecessary harm to some of our most vulnerable families.

But it also means thinking beyond TANF, toward a progressive agenda tied to work that emphasizes the public obligation that should come with personal responsibility. We have framed these policies in terms of earnings and work supports, but it is early enough in the debate to begin this dialogue in earnest; new ideas may surface. Our hope is that a coalition will form—a coalition composed of those affected directly by the policy, their advocates, and their political representatives. Armed with a balanced view of TANF's impact that is based on the evidence thus far, and with a policy agenda targeted both at and beyond TANF, such a coalition can make a real and lasting difference in the lives of working Americans.

*"Poverty [is] best attacked by the policy of
mandatory work supplemented by
government work supports."*

Work Requirements and Government Subsidies Will Reduce Poverty

Ron Haskins

Ending the guaranteed entitlement to cash benefits for poor single parents, the 1996 welfare reform law imposed a two-year limit on public assistance, after which welfare recipients are required to work. In the following viewpoint, Ron Haskins asserts that work requirements, often referred to as "welfare-to-work," have reduced child poverty and promoted responsible work habits among the poor. As the welfare law comes up for congressional reauthorization in 2002, Haskins maintains that Congress should continue its support system of benefits such as subsidized housing and tax credits for low-income working families in order to lift them out of poverty. The author is a senior fellow in the Brookings Institution, an independent public policy organization.

As you read, consider the following questions:
1. By what percentage have the welfare rolls declined since their peak in the spring of 1994, according to the author?
2. According to Haskins, how does the Census Bureau's official poverty measure understate the progress the nation is making against child poverty?

The essence of the 1996 welfare reform law was work. Under the new law, welfare recipients, previously subject to only loose requirements of any type, were to be strongly encouraged—even forced—to work. The legal entitlement to cash welfare was to be ended in favor of a system that required work and other signs of personal responsibility as a condition of receiving benefits. Previous welfare law had paid lip service to work but had imposed no work requirements for single mothers. For those few welfare recipients selected to meet a work participation standard, such as education, the law had exacted few consequences for failure. But in 1996, and even earlier as some states began to impose work requirements by obtaining waivers from federal law, the requirement to work became real. Recipients who refused to work or prepare for work had their benefits reduced; more than 30 states adopted sanction policy that terminated benefits completely. States that did not place a specific percentage of their recipients in work or work preparation programs suffered financial penalties. Recipients were also subjected to a five-year limit on benefits, a strong signal that self-support is a must.

From Welfare to Work

Coupled with a booming economy and public policies to help the working poor, these tough reforms have been associated with an historic decline in the welfare rolls—more than 50 percent from the peak welfare enrollment of 5.1 million families in the spring of 1994. So mothers are leaving welfare in record numbers. But are they finding work?

Brookings economist Gary Burtless has shown, using national employment data from the Census Bureau, that after a decade of stagnation at about 57–58 percent, the employment rate of single mothers increased slightly in 1994 and then shot up dramatically every year between 1995 and 1999 to 72 percent, an all-time high. More remarkable still, the employment rate of never-married mothers, who are the most likely to have little education or job experience and long stays on welfare, increased even more. Between 1992 and 1996, their employment rate rose gradually from around 43 percent to 49 percent. But in the three years after enactment of the 1996 legislation, the rate exploded. By 1999 it had risen to 65 percent, also an all-time high and an increase of 33 percent in just three years.

Is Poverty Falling?

Virtually everyone in the policy world agrees that since the 1996 reforms were enacted, welfare rolls have fallen dramatically and employment by female family heads, especially never-married heads, has risen impressively. But most observers are not satisfied with declines in welfare and increased work. They want to know if the mothers and children formerly on welfare are financially better off.

Of the many measures that could be picked to examine financial well-being, one of the most useful is the poverty measure used by the U.S. Census Bureau. Although not without its critics, the measure stands out as a reasonable means to trace changes in family material well-being for two reasons. First, it is widely used by social scientists, reporters, and politicians. Second, it has been computed in a standard manner that produces a continuous data series on poverty from 1959 to 1999.

Figure 1 compares the annual percentage change in the welfare caseload, the Census Bureau measure of child poverty, and the Census Bureau measure of black child poverty during 1995–99. All three measures fell every year. Even the smallest annual decline in the welfare rolls during those five years, around 7 percent in 1995, exceeds those of any year before 1995, highlighting the historic nature of the decline in cash welfare.

The declines in overall child poverty and black child poverty are also impressive. Not only did both rates decline every year, but the black child poverty rate has been falling for seven straight years, the most sustained decline since the Census Bureau began measuring it in 1974. Further, the declines in black child poverty in 1997 and 1999, 6.8 percent and 9.8 percent respectively, are the largest ever recorded, and the rate today is the lowest it has ever been. In fact, between 1974 and 1992, the general drift of black child poverty was up. Over this 17-year period, as Congress greatly increased spending on welfare programs, poverty among black children fell in nine years and grew in eight; overall the rate increased from 39.9 percent to 46.6 percent, well over 15 percent. Indeed, during the prolonged economic expansion of the 1980s, as the American economy added nearly 20 million jobs, black child poverty never fell below 43.1 percent, as compared with 33.1 percent in 1999.

Figure 1: Decline in Welfare Caseloads and Child Poverty

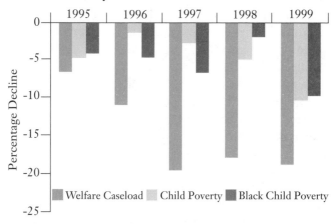

Caseload data from Congressional Research Services, poverty data from U.S. Census Bureau.

Despite this historic progress against poverty, the Census Bureau's official poverty measure understates the progress the nation is now making against child poverty because it does not take into account in-kind federal benefits (such as food stamps) or tax benefits (such as the earned income tax credit [EITC]) for which low-income working families generally qualify. Indeed, by not counting these two benefits alone, the official poverty measure ignores at least $35 billion in benefits enjoyed by low-income working families. Fortunately, the Census Bureau also publishes an experimental poverty measure that includes these and a few similar benefits like housing. Figure 2 uses this alternative measure to show the true progress the nation made in reducing children's poverty during the economic expansions of the 1980s and the 1990s. In both expansions, child poverty declined. But it fell more than twice as much during the 1990s as during the 1980s—35.5 percent as against 15.5 percent.

Two developments explain the vast differences in poverty reduction during the two decades. But before examining them, I address one widely cited factor in explaining the difference—namely, the economy. During the boom of the 1980s, the American economy added a net of almost 20 million jobs. If, as many analysts and pundits claim, a hot economy plucks people off welfare, then we would expect the welfare rolls to have declined during the 1980s. But let's look at the data. When the economy first began adding jobs in the spring of 1983, the welfare rolls were growing. As the economy added a net of about 1 million jobs over the next year, they continued to climb. Between 1984 and the winter of 1988, as the economy added another 9 million jobs, the welfare rolls remained relatively flat, moving up and down in no apparent pattern. By 1988, they stood at about 3.7 million families, about the same as at the beginning of recovery in 1983 when a total of 16 million fewer Americans held jobs. Then over the next 18 months, as the economy added another 3 million jobs, the rolls shot up nearly 12 percent to more than 4 million families. During the entire 1980s expansion, the American economy added 20 million jobs and the welfare rolls grew by nearly half a million families. Those who want to attribute the recent remarkable decline in welfare rolls to the booming economy of the 1990s must account for why an economy that was almost as superb during the 1980s failed to reduce, and on the contrary, was associated with an actual increase in welfare rolls.

What Made the 1990s Different?

The 1990s have been a different story. For the first two-plus years of the recovery, between roughly December 1991 and March 1994, as the economy added about 6 million jobs, the welfare rolls grew by a surprising 700,000 families. But then, as more than half the states implemented work programs by 1994 and especially after enactment of the sweeping federal welfare reform legislation in 1996, the welfare rolls began a sustained decline that has yet to stop. Even more interesting, the nation is also in a sustained period during which poverty is declining more sharply than at any time since the 1950s.

Here's why. First, the mandatory work requirements out-lined above spurred people to leave welfare and take jobs. Before the 1996 reforms, families accumulated on the wel-fare rolls and stayed for long spells. In fact, the average stay, counting repeat spells, for families on the rolls at any given moment was a shocking 12 years. Thus, even though the economy might expand rapidly, as it did during the 1980s, most families on welfare could not possibly benefit from the rising opportunity because they weren't even in the job mar-ket. And public policy did not encourage or, where neces-sary, force them into the job market. In the 1990s, by con-trast, in large part because of the much more demanding welfare system, many families who would have been on wel-fare in previous years entered the job market and found jobs.

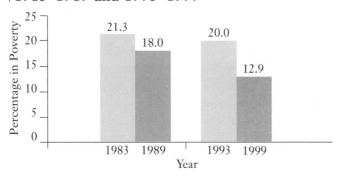

Figure 2: Child Poverty, Including In-Kind Government Benefits and Tax Benefits, 1983–1989 and 1993–1999

U.S. Census Bureau.

But the jobs they found generally paid low wages. So how did so many of them escape poverty? The answer brings us to the second cause for the great drop in poverty during the 1990s. Since roughly 1985, Congress has been quietly build-ing a work support system that provides public benefits for low-income working families, especially those with children. This work support system includes housing, food stamps, the earned income tax credit, Medicaid, the Child Health Insurance Program, the child tax credit, child care, child support enforcement, and a variety of nutrition benefits for children such as school lunch, food subsidies for day care, and a major food program for mothers and infants. All have one feature in common: working families can receive benefits as long as their income is below a cut-off point that varies by program but is quite high. For example, the cut-off for food stamps is around $18,000; that for the EITC is more than $29,000. Thus, a mother with two children leaving welfare and earning $10,000 a year can supplement her income by $4,000 in cash from the EITC and by more than $2,000 in food stamps, bringing her total pre-tax income to $16,000 and lifting her and her children out of poverty.

Build on Success

As the time approaches to reauthorize the 1996 welfare reform legislation, it is important that members of Congress, their staffs, and the public realize how successful the 1996 legislation has been in reducing poverty. Although Congress created scores of new programs and increased spending by billions of dollars in the decades leading up to welfare reform, no progress was made against children's poverty. Government action in simply giving away money, in-kind benefits, and social services—some on an entitlement basis—turned out to be a lousy way to reduce poverty. But the 1996 legislation marks a departure from providing guaranteed benefits to an approach demanding individual responsibility and then providing public subsidies for work. The result is historic declines in welfare, increases in work, and declines in poverty.

To continue and even expand this new approach, both liberals and conservatives must recognize that their favorite solutions to poverty are inadequate. Giving people benefits leaves them in poverty, reduces their propensity to work, and arguably impedes family formation. But pushing people to leave welfare for work does not ensure that they and their families will avoid poverty. Such are the work skills of millions of American parents that the value of their labor in the market is inadequate to support a family. In view of this stubborn reality, the best strategy is to require work and then provide public subsidies that lift working families out of poverty. As experience since the seminal 1996 reforms shows so clearly, only the combination of work and work subsidies will both promote personal responsibility and effectively fight poverty. At last, after three decades of failing to help families leave poverty by giving them lots of cash and in-kind welfare, we have found that both material and behavioral poverty are best attacked by the policy of mandatory work supplemented by government work supports.

> *"Instead of trying to reform poor mothers to become working poor mothers, we need to take a closer look at . . . what it will take to make work possible for mothers who support families."*

Work Requirements Harm Poor Mothers

Randy Albelda

Randy Albelda argues in the following viewpoint that the current policy of requiring the head of each welfare family to work within two years of accepting benefits is harming poor mothers and their children. According to Albelda, work requirements are pushing women into inflexible, low-wage jobs that offer no health benefits and inadequate support for raising children. The present welfare policy should be amended to include income supplements for part-time work or a shorter work week, so that mothers do not have to put low-wage employment ahead of the needs of their children. Albelda is a professor of economics at the University of Massachusetts, Boston.

As you read, consider the following questions:
1. According to the author, what factors impede the entry of welfare mothers into the labor market?
2. How does the "obsession" with employment for poor mothers in welfare reform represent a major change in thinking about women and public assistance, according to Albelda?

"Ending welfare as we know it" has rapidly become ending welfare. Time limits virtually assure that the majority of families who receive welfare will be cut off at least from federal funding. The current trend is to replace welfare with earnings and is best summed up by the ever-present term "welfare-to-work."

The welfare-to-work "solution" can be thought of as a match made in hell. It puts poor mothers who need the most support and flexibility into jobs in the low-wage labor market which often are the most inflexible, have the least family-necessary benefits (vacation time, health care, sick days), and provide levels of pay that often are insufficient to support a single person, let alone a family. This mismatch is not going to be resolved by providing short-term job training, work vans, poor-quality child care, or even refundable earned income tax credits. It is a political, social, and economic problem that must be addressed in our policies but also in our national psyche. It starts with valuing the work that families do. Raising children—in any and all family configurations—is absolutely vital work to our individual and collective well-being. And it is deserving. Recognizing this will not only transform how we think about welfare, it can and must change how we think about the structure of paid work. We must have access to paid work that allows us to take care of our families and have a family life without relegating all women to the home.

Been There, Done That

Ending welfare poses some historically familiar alternatives for women. Getting married and staying married—thus being dependent on a man—was of course the fond hope and major inspiration for conservatives who sponsored the 1996 Personal Responsibility and Work Opportunity Reconciliation Act (PRWORA). The Act leads with these two "findings": 1) Marriage is the foundation of a successful society; and 2) Marriage is an essential institution of a successful society which promotes the interests of children.

The path most proponents of welfare reform promote publicly, however, is "welfare-to-work." There is a wide range of methods for promoting paid work instead of welfare, from the punitive "work-first" strategies pursued by over half the states to the more liberal strategies (which include a generous package of training and education options, day care, transportation, and health care) put forth by Mary Jo Bane and David Ellwood when they were welfare reform policymakers in the Clinton Administration. Despite its current popularity, the notion of putting welfare mothers to "work" is hardly new. Work requirements have long been part of Aid to Families with Dependent Children (AFDC), and were seen as an important way to get women, particularly black women, off the welfare rolls. It was only in the early 1990s, however, that paid work became the main alternative in light of benefit time limits.

Most states, as well as the ancillary not-for-profit agencies and for-profit companies that get lucrative welfare-related contracts, are putting significant energies into getting adult welfare recipients to "work." Work in this case means paid employment or unpaid community or public-service placements (workfare). But there are problems with welfare-to-work, some of which states readily recognize and are working to cope with (however inadequately), and others which states do not even recognize.

Inadequate Supports for Welfare-to-Work Moms

One aspect of states' welfare-to-work policy has always been their concern with the "job readiness" of welfare mothers. From vast amounts of published research we know many welfare mothers have low educational attainment and many lack recent job experience (although the vast majority have been employed at some point). Both of these characteristics impede entry into the labor market and, once there, all but assure low wages. This is too bad since welfare-to-work ideology rests on short-term training, which is reinforced by precluding most education from qualifying as "work-related activities" in the work quotas established in PRWORA. This of course means that many state programs will be ineffectual in improving women's skills.

More and more research is uncovering another set of barriers to work, including learning disabilities, severe bouts of depression, and experiences with domestic violence. The prediction is that the easy-to-place recipients will soon be thrown out of the welfare system and those who remain will require much more training and support to get paid employment. Ironically, or perhaps cynically, welfare will become exactly how it was portrayed for years—a system that serves very low-functioning women with children who need long-term assistance. Recent studies show that over 41% of current recipients have less than a high school diploma, and between 10% and 31% of welfare recipients are currently victims of domestic violence. Helping women overcome barriers to employment will take time, quality counseling, and long-term training, something welfare reform is discouraging or prohibiting.

Monthly Earnings of Welfare Recipients* Who Find Employment

Area Studied	Monthly Earnings	As a Percent of Federal Poverty Line
Los Angeles	$695	67%
Delaware	$705	66%
Escambia County, Florida	$682	65%
Michigan	$907	90%
Minnesota (five urban counties)	$699	67%
Portland, Oregon	$712	70%

*Including those no longer receiving assistance and those combining welfare and work

Note: The types of families included and time periods involved varied between the geographic areas. Years are 1996 and/or 1997 except for Portland, which was 1993 to 1994.

What distinguishes welfare recipients from other poor people is that two thirds of them are children being raised, most often, by a mother on her own. Welfare has always been a program for families with young children. Therefore, welfare-to-work requires a substantial set of ancillary supports that mothers with small children need to get to work, such as health insurance, transportation, and child care. Since many jobs available to welfare-to-work mothers do not provide health insurance, states allow women to stay on Medicaid, but typically only for one year after leaving welfare. Then they're on their own. Some states have recognized the transportation challenge mothers face—efficiently getting children to and from day care and school, and getting themselves to and from work in a timely fashion—and some are trying to solve this problem with loaner cars, work vans, and public transportation vouchers. In rural and suburban areas, however, the problems are much more difficult since adequate transportation is just not there. Regarding child care, policy makers recognize the need for it, but their solutions should make us shiver. Very few states pay any attention to the quality of care. Any care seems to do for poor mothers. In Massachusetts, for example, the state encourages mothers to find low-cost caretakers with reimbursements of $15 a day. Assuming you get what you pay for, such child care is a disaster for mothers and children. Moreover, it impoverishes and exploits the caregivers.

And What About the Problems with No Name?

Will welfare-to-work actually ensure economic "independence"? Many are avoiding this question because the economic expansion, which has both accompanied and accommodated welfare-to-work, has at least fulfilled one premise of welfare reform—moving women from the rolls to a job. However, come the downturn, many who did get jobs will lose them and caseloads will creep back up. Further, the expansion has allowed states to be slack, if not entirely unimaginative, in their training and education efforts, relying on the economic expansion to reduce rolls and thereby claim victory in the welfare reform battle.

Will finding a job mean earning a living wage? Not likely. What is almost always ignored or conveniently forgotten in the blind faith that all too often accompanies the welfare-to-work mentality is that the U.S. labor market has always failed women who have little formal education and sporadic job experiences. Women have a very hard time supporting themselves, let alone families, on wages from waitressing, sales clerking, cleaning hotel rooms, or even assisting administrators. Yet these are exactly the kinds of jobs welfare-to-work mothers are likely to get.

In addition to the problems of a fickle labor market and

chronically low wages, women in the welfare-to-work pipeline must cope with the fact that most jobs are not "mother ready." That is, they do not accommodate mothers' needs, even when training, work, and child care arrangements are in place. These are not unknown or new needs. They include the remarkably mundane events such as children getting sick, school and medical appointments, school vacations, and early-release school days. Employers, especially those who employ low-wage workers, do not want workers who come in late because a school bus didn't show up, miss days because there was no child care, or worry about their children at 3:00 P.M.—instead of doing their tedious low-wage-earning tasks. Unfortunately, low-wage employers of current and former welfare recipients are least likely to grant sick leave and vacation time. According to a report in last year's *American Journal of Public Health*, 46% of women who had never been on welfare got sick leave and vacation pay at their jobs, as compared to 24% of women who had been on welfare less than two years, and 19% of women who had been on welfare more than two years.

Most state administrators, politicians, journalists, and researchers see the work of taking care of children as a cost of welfare-to-work, but not as an important and valuable family activity. Devaluing women's unpaid work in the home is clearly evident in studies of welfare reform. Typically, researchers compare welfare families' and employed families' material well-being without imputing any value to women's time. In short, the value of women's unpaid labor in the home when she is receiving welfare is zero. As a policy, welfare-to-work fails to grapple with the fact that adults responsible for children cannot (and probably should not) put their jobs—especially low-wage ones—before the needs of their children.

Family Values/Valuing Families

The ideologues who concern themselves with poor mothers exhibit split personalities when it comes to getting women to work. The conservative architects of welfare reform who want to force poor mothers to do lousy jobs are now busy enacting tax cuts to encourage middle-class moms to stay at home and trying hard to eliminate the "marriage penalty" in the tax code. Liberals, on the other hand, seem preoccupied with providing inadequate supports for full-time employment for poor mothers. What's going on?

One way to make sense of the obsession with employment for poor mothers is to see the emphasis on paid work in welfare reform as a major change in thinking about women and public assistance. Indeed, it is a major value shift. The Social Security Act of 1935 made all poor single mothers entitled to receive AFDC, although the levels received were far lower than the other two major programs (Social Security and Unemployment Insurance) in that historic legislation. At that time, the notion of having to "work" for one's benefits was not an expectation of most single mothers. Women who were not attached to male breadwinners received income, but not much.

Another old value set guiding single mothers' receipt of cash assistance pivoted on how women became single mothers. Widows were seen as deserving, while divorced, separated, and never-married mothers were not. Benefit levels reinforced these "values."

What makes a single mother "deserving" today has changed. The salient factor is no longer how she happened to become a single parent, but rather if she is engaged in paid labor. This sentiment is only possible in an age when most women are in the paid labor market and when the moral repugnance of women without men has dissipated. Ironically, both of these accomplishments can be attributed in part to the successes of the women's movement, coupled with modern industrialization. As more and more women are drawn into the labor force, they tend to have fewer children and are not as likely to get or stay married. Interestingly, both conservatives and liberals have lent weight to the idea that working single mothers are more deserving.

The positive value of employment was accompanied by the negative value placed on receiving welfare. Led by Ronald Reagan and conservative thinker Charles Murray in the 1980s, welfare opponents referred to AFDC recipients as "welfare queens." They were presumed to have loads of children, leach resources from the state, and then pass their dysfunctional behavior on to their children. In the mid-1980s through the 1990s, many "liberal" poverty researchers carried this banner as well. "Underclass" authors, notably William Julius Wilson and Christopher Jencks, as well as their Left detractors, such as William Darity and Samuel Myers, discussed welfare receipt as a pathology—one of the many "bad" behaviors that helps reproduce poverty. Jencks even referred to women receiving welfare as the "reproductive underclass." Further, when adult recipients have earnings, even if they receive hefty supplements, they are not perceived as receiving "hand-outs" and hence are deserving. It would seem, then, putting welfare mothers to work solves the problem of growing welfare rolls and plays into American values that will help restore safety nets for the poor. On both the Right and the Left, putting poor mothers to work is the prescribed cure to their "dysfunctional" tendencies.

A Progressive Agenda

I do not want to argue here that paid work is bad. Indeed, earnings can and do buy economic security and some independence from men, especially from abusive relationships. In a society that values paid work, doing it can build your self-esteem as well. However, welfare-to-work is a setup. The types of jobs poor mothers get and can keep provide neither much dignity nor sufficient wages. Working enough hours at low wages to support a family is often untenable. Women fail too often. This is not only demoralizing, but economically debilitating. If we don't think both about valuing women's work at home as well as when they do paid work, welfare-to-work is a cruel hoax that makes legislators feel better about themselves, but leaves poor families in the lurch.

Instead of trying to reform poor mothers to become working poor mothers, we need to take a closer look at job structures and what it will take to make work possible for mothers who support families. This might include a shorter work week or at least income supplements to those who take a part-time job so that families can still pay for basic needs like housing, health insurance, child care, food, and clothing. Paid family and medical leave and expanded unemployment insurance to cover less continuous and low-paying part-time work must also be in place. A mother shouldn't lose her job or her weekly pay because her child gets chicken pox. Herein lies the true opportunity of welfare-to-work welfare reform. . . .

A national discussion about the value of women's work in the home is much needed for all women, not just those who turn to public assistance. It would raise several important sets of policy issues, including:

• seriously considering the provision of publicly funded family care such as child care centers, extended day programs, and child allowances;

• working to make sure that welfare is not punitive, and is at least comparable to social security and unemployment insurance; and

• focusing not just on making mothers "job ready," but promoting policies that make paid work "mother-ready"— in other words, conducive to mothers' needs, paying a living wage, and offering opportunities for advancement.

If we as a nation recognized the value of women's work, we wouldn't have welfare reform that merely replaces public assistance with forcing mothers into working jobs at low wages and a shallow set of supports that vanishes quickly. Seeing the work of raising children as a benefit to society, not merely a cost of going to work, would mean developing a welfare-to-work regime that truly supports part-time waged work. Further, it might make us more cognizant that for some families at some points in their lives, having the sole adult in the labor force is not possible or desirable. Public income supports for poor single mothers will always need to exist precisely because we value the work of mothers taking care of their children.

"The logical way to eliminate dependence [on welfare] . . . is to adopt a prohibition against new, single mothers' signing onto the rolls."

Welfare Policies Should Discourage Out-of-Wedlock Births

Lisa E. Oliphant

Many critics contend that the welfare system promotes illegitimate births and dependency by giving unmarried mothers cash benefits. In addressing this problem, the 1996 welfare reform law places restrictions on benefits to unwed teen parents, and it allows states to deny additional benefits to families having more children while receiving assistance. In the following viewpoint, Lisa E. Oliphant contends that welfare reform has not gone far enough to discourage out-of-wedlock births and divert families away from public assistance. In the author's opinion, the most effective way to end unmarried mothers' dependency on welfare is to prohibit new single mothers from signing onto the welfare rolls. Oliphant is an entitlements policy analyst at the Cato Institute, a conservative research organization.

As you read, consider the following questions:
1. In the author's opinion, why do potential recipients have little reason to fear losing welfare benefits?
2. What impact has the welfare reform law had on the number of illegitimate births, according to Oliphant?
3. According to the author, how should families be "diverted" from signing onto the welfare rolls?

Excerpted from "Four Years of Welfare Reform: A Progress Report," by Lisa E. Oliphant, *Cato Institute Policy Analysis*, August 22, 2000. Copyright © 2000 by the Cato Institute. Reprinted with permission.

Welfare reform's progress to date has shown the new law's limited impact on individuals already entrenched in the system. Most former recipients are no worse off—in fact, they are often better off—because of the new legislation, but only a small fraction no longer needs, or appears to be on the path to not needing, means-tested assistance. Welfare reform, as envisioned by the drafters of the 1996 law, appears incapable of fully freeing recipients from the grips of dependence. Nearly four years after enactment of the Personal Responsibility and Work Opportunity Reconciliation Act (PRWORA), we are left with a working welfare state that engenders a new form of dependence on supplemental assistance.

More Spending Leads to More Families on Welfare

As Michael Tanner of the Cato Institute has suggested, the best way to end dependence is, not through curative efforts, but to prevent its onset in the first place. He warned in 1996 that

> there are serious problems with expecting hard-core, long-term welfare recipients to be able to find sufficient employment to support themselves and their families. When we established the incentives of the current system, we may have made a Faustian bargain with those recipients. Now it may be too late to change the rules of the game. We should do whatever we can to move those people out of the system but recognize that success may be limited. It is far more important to prevent anyone new from becoming trapped in the system.

Welfare reformers' efforts to slow entry into the system largely involve provisions aimed at tackling teenage and out-of-wedlock births. Those attempts, however, are being diluted by the states' eagerness to spend more on welfare than they did before the new legislation. There is little reason for potential recipients to fear a rolling back of the safety net when, as of 1998, almost all states had increased spending per welfare family and nearly half were spending more than required by the new law. Of the 35 states that had increased spending by 30 percent or more per welfare family, 16 had increased spending by 50 percent or more, and 3 had actually doubled the amount spent per family. As the U.S. Department of Health & Human Services (HHS) has observed, "Overall, based both on the level of spending in FY 98 reported by States and on the cash assistance levels established by the States under the Temporary Assistance for Needy Families (TANF) program, there is clearly no 'race to the bottom' occurring." The explosion in welfare spending over the last four years is a likely reason for major setbacks in efforts to reduce out-of-wedlock childbearing by young women.

Reducing Out-of-Wedlock Births

Having a child out of wedlock is often a precursor to a lifetime of poverty and dependence. Out-of-wedlock pregnancy, in fact, is the reason that one-third of welfare recipients end up on the rolls and is the cause of most long-term dependence. Studies suggest that the availability of welfare, ironically, is largely to blame for the fact that the number of out-of-wedlock births has increased by more than 600 percent and the rate of births to unmarried teenagers has quadrupled over the past four decades. As Tanner explains, "By removing the economic consequences of out-of-wedlock births, welfare has removed a major incentive to avoid them." "Responsible behavior," says Ben Wattenberg of the American Enterprise Institute, "rises in reaction to a lack of viable irresponsible economic alternatives and to the cessation of messages by governments that out-of-wedlock birth is a socially acceptable lifestyle."

Welfare reformers claim to have taken illegitimacy seriously when drafting the new law. In order to continue to receive federal TANF funding, states must (1) restrict benefits to unwed teen parents under 18 who do not live at home and attend school and (2) outline how they intend to establish goals and act to prevent and reduce the number of nonmarital pregnancies—particularly those of teenagers. To further discourage teen pregnancy, the new law also allows states to institute a "family cap" that denies additional benefits to families to which more children are born while the family is receiving assistance. Finally, the new law offers bonuses to the five states that rank highest in decreasing out-of-wedlock births while also decreasing abortion.

Illegitimate Births Continue to Rise

Unfortunately, as the *New York Times* reports, illegitimacy is "a front on which progress has been slight if at all." The new welfare law has been particularly ineffective in curbing out-of-wedlock births to teenagers—those whom lawmakers most hoped to target. Between 1993 and 1997, when states first began experimenting with welfare reform, the percentage of all births that were to unmarried teenagers (the teenage illegitimacy ratio) rose by as much as 28 percent in every state except Rhode Island. By 1997, in five states more than 90 percent of teen mothers were unmarried. Over the last few years, the percentage of all births that is to unmarried teens has continued to rise, though at a slightly slower pace. When the entire pool of single mothers is considered, welfare reform's impact on illegitimacy is even less impressive. PRWORA has had no measurable impact on the overall ratio of out-of-wedlock to married-couple births. As Figure 1 shows, after nearly doubling between 1980 and 1994, the proportion of American babies being born to unmarried women has remained relatively constant at about one-third of all births in recent years. The actual number of out-of-wedlock births to black women has been declining, but that trend began in 1989, before the states and the federal government began enacting welfare reform measures, and the percentage of illegitimate births to black women has remained steady.

Reducing Teen Pregnancy

Like unwed motherhood, teenage pregnancy is strongly linked with subsequent welfare dependence. More than three-quarters of unwed teen mothers end up on welfare before their children reach school age. In recognition of the relationship between teen pregnancy and dependence, the new welfare law, in addition to requiring unmarried teen mothers to stay at home and remain in school, contains several provisions aimed specifically at pregnancy prevention. PRWORA allocates $50 million annually to abstinence education, requires establishment of national teen pregnancy prevention goals, and mandates that at least 25 percent of U.S. communities have teen pregnancy prevention programs in place. The HHS recently claimed, "The strategy sends the strongest possible message to all teens that postponing sexual activity, staying in school, and preparing for work are the right things to do."

Has this message worked its magic? Welfare reformers can hardly contain their excitement over recent dramatic declines in the teen birth rate, as well as in the number of second births to teenage mothers. Inspection of those figures, however, reveals more modest progress in reducing births to teenagers, a dubious connection between the downward trend and specific provisions of the new welfare law, and sobering evidence that illegitimate births to teens remain an inexorable challenge.

Figure 1: Out-of-Wedlock Births as Percentage of All Births, 1980–99

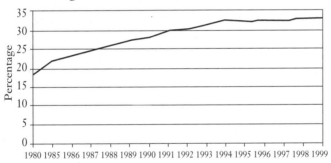

Lisa E. Oliphant, *Cato Institute Policy Analysis*, August 22, 2000.

Progress in reducing the number of births to teens has been less impressive than national figures tend to convey. Critics note, for instance, inconsistent (and often lagging) progress among the states. Child Trends points out that whereas Vermont has reduced teen pregnancy to 11 births per 1,000 teens, states like Mississippi lag behind at 58 births per 1,000 teens. Supporters of the new welfare law also cite the decline in the percentage of teenage mothers who have second children as evidence that the welfare law has succeeded in dissuading those women from having more children. The supporters note, for instance, that the percentage of teenage mothers going on to have a second child decreased between 1993 and 1997. What critics say they fail to point out, however, is that, two years into welfare reform, the number of teenage mothers who had second pregnancies began to level off at around 22 percent and has shown no further sign of inching downward.

Casting Doubt on Reform's Effects

The declines in teen pregnancy that have occurred, however, certainly represent progress over the last decade. Nevertheless, several facts cast doubt on the relationship between this hopeful trend and welfare reform. First, note critics, the impressive downward trend in the teen pregnancy rate began long before welfare reform measures were instituted. Second, while the thrust of the new law's attack on teen pregnancy has been abstinence education, much of the decline in teen pregnancies, says Child Trends' Jennifer Manlove, is attributable to increased use of injectible contraceptives. She points out: "There has been little rigorous research on the effectiveness of abstinence-only programs. Consequently, the jury is still out on whether abstinence programs can significantly reduce teen childbearing." Third, it is difficult to discern the link between programs intended to prevent teen pregnancy in general and teen birth rates, says the General Accounting Office (GAO), because, while the states are tracking changes in teen birth rates, few are actually evaluating the effects of their prevention programs on teen pregnancy.

More important than the scale and cause of the declines, however, is the fact that fewer teenage pregnancies over the last few years do not appear to be associated with fewer young women bearing children out of wedlock. It is not teenage pregnancy, per se, that presages welfare dependence but the choice by the majority of young mothers to give birth out of wedlock. If, as has been the case since welfare reform, the number of teenagers having children has inched downward, but the overall percentage of births that occur to unmarried mothers has remained steady or continued to climb, then the primary precursor to welfare dependence has not been tackled.

For those who have already become pregnant as teenagers or out-of-wedlock, or both, how viable an alternative does welfare remain under the new law? As we have seen, once women become part of the system, it becomes very difficult to fully escape it, despite the range of work-support measures and incentives created by PRWORA. An important goal of welfare reform should thus be preventing the onset of dependence by "diverting" families from signing onto the rolls in the first place. As Professor June O'Neill of City University of New York told the Subcommittee on Human Resources of the House Committee on Ways and Means in 1999, "Although attention is usually focused on the effects of the policy changes on welfare leaver rates, the ultimate efficacy of welfare reform is going to turn on the extent to which it will have changed the incentive structures in the program, and whether that change is enough to deter young women from entering in the first place."

As of August 1998, 35 states were employing some form of "diversion" tactic aimed particularly at those considered "job ready" or who had another potential source of income, including

- urging applicants to ask for help from relatives instead of signing up for government assistance,

- writing one-time emergency checks or offering low-interest loans in place of monthly benefits,

- referring individuals to private charities, and

- requiring applicants to spend weeks searching for work before they receive their first welfare payment.

The HHS identifies three specific types of diversion programs being tried throughout the country. "Lump-sum payment" programs make available a one-time payment to families with a short-term financial need; "mandatory applicant job search" programs require job searches as a condition of TANF eligibility, with the aim of encouraging individuals to secure employment before receiving the first welfare check; and "alternative resources exploration" encourages families to consider other forms of support from family and community as a substitute for cash assistance from the state. As of 1997, the HHS reports 20 states were employing the "lump-sum payment" tactic, 16 states were requiring "mandatory applicant job search," and only 7 states were using an aggressive "alternative resources" approach. Only three states had implemented all three types of diversion strategies.

To what extent do decreasing TANF claims reflect the success of diversion policies in causing fewer people to enter the system in the first place? The *Washington Post* suggests that "the combination of these and similar [diversion tactics] explains a significant portion of the decline in welfare caseloads. . . . One noted researcher believes the policies are responsible for one-third of the . . . drop in caseloads since the nation's welfare system was overhauled in 1996. . . . The new tactic is critical to understanding the remarkable decline in the number of Americans receiving welfare over the past two years. While many poor families have moved off public assistance and into jobs, many others simply have never gone on the rolls." In 1999 the GAO agreed that "states' diverting eligible families from receiving cash assistance may have contributed to the large decline," and the Committee for Economic Development remarked earlier this year that "the overall rate at which new welfare cases join the rolls has fallen sharply." In states aggressively pursuing diversion strategies, such as Florida and Kentucky, the percentage of applicants who end up on the rolls has decreased by as much as 20 percent.

The Importance of Prevention

In general, it appears that welfare reform, through diversion, has made important strides in preventing individuals from becoming first-time recipients of cash assistance. Nevertheless, the gates to TANF remain open for individuals who are incapable of working, have no alternative source of income or support, or require more than a one-time check to bridge the time between jobs. This is where prevention of out-of-wedlock births to young women becomes particularly important. Once an unmarried young woman decides to have children, she usually becomes a valid candidate for TANF receipt—someone unlikely to be turned away during the diversion phase, or, as they call it in the United Kingdom, the "Gateway" to welfare. Diversion is instrumental mainly in weeding out individuals who are in transition and show potential for becoming self-supporting or have access to alternative means of support. It can do little for those who have chosen poorly and consequently condemned themselves and their families to a lifetime of dependence.

The Real Solution: Stopping Dependence

Pulling dependent families out of the "poverty trap" has proven a formidable task for welfare reformers. Many recipients have little education or work experience and are trying to raise families without the help of a spouse. A fast-food job and food stamps, plus short-term counseling and training classes, usually can't do much in the long term for families that, until now, have gotten by with the help of a welfare check. The real solution involves stopping such dependence before it is given a chance, with the help of cash assistance, to flourish.

Welfare reformers know that prevention is important. Measures to decrease out-of-wedlock births, teen pregnancy, and first-time welfare claims constitute an important portion of the 1996 welfare law. Unfortunately, the results associated with those measures do not, on the whole, make up a significant portion of welfare reform's success story. Illegitimate births remain a significant problem, particularly among young mothers, and have not shown any recent signs of inching downward. In addition, it is difficult to establish a link between advances in reducing out-of-wedlock and teenage births and measures enacted under the new law.

Diversion strategies applied as a result of welfare reform have shown some success in turning new applicants toward alternative means of support. Though that represents a positive development in and of itself, there is no evidence that diversion strategies are effective as a disincentive for those, such as unwed teens or high-school dropouts, thinking of choosing life-long dependence. Women who have no other means of support or who are unable to work remain, even under diversion policies, key candidates for welfare receipt. Increased spending on recipients under the new law, moreover, makes welfare seem that much more viable an alternative for at-risk women. Prevention, in practice, has not been the resounding message of welfare reform.

Too Much of a Safety Net

Consider the particular provisions of the 1996 welfare law in light of Wattenberg's comment that putting an end to the country's unwed teenage pregnancy problem requires the dismantling of "viable irresponsible economic alternatives" and "the cessation of messages by governments" that such choices lead to a "socially acceptable lifestyle." As we have seen, lack of progress in tackling out-of-wedlock pregnancy may indicate that welfare reform has not gone far enough in making welfare a less appealing and viable alternative. Far from eliminating welfare, the new law may be sending contradictory messages by continuing to spend generously on current recipients. Potential young single mothers, despite the changed rules, may continue to get pregnant, believing that in no way has the safety net actually been dismantled. And, in a very important sense, they are correct. As we have seen, the new federal TANF block grant created by welfare reform enables states that reduce their caseloads to provide a more generous array of support to each remaining welfare family, including continued cash benefits, intensive counseling, subsidized work, and transportation assistance. The problem, aside from the fact that the extra support does not appear to have been very effective in assisting those who face multiple obstacles to becoming independent, is that such spending may convey to potential young recipients the message that a fortified and ever-present safety net awaits them if they should choose to become pregnant out of wedlock.

The logical way to eliminate dependence and its various causes, which Tanner proposed before the new law was enacted, is to adopt a prohibition against new, single mothers' signing onto the rolls. If welfare were eliminated for those women, Tanner predicts, out-of-wedlock births as a percentage of all births would likely decline by between 15 and 50 percent.

*"Adopting [welfare] policies that . . .
discriminat[e] against female-headed families
in favor of married couples is unfair."*

Welfare Policies Should Not Promote Marriage

Laurie Rubiner

To discourage poor women from having children out of wedlock and joining the welfare rolls, the 1996 welfare reform law restricts the benefits available to unwed teen parents and provides federal bonuses to states that decrease out-of-wedlock births. In the following viewpoint, Laurie Rubiner contends that legislation to reauthorize the welfare reform law in 2002 must avoid coercive policies that penalize families for not conforming to the two-parent structure preferred by conservative lawmakers. Promoting marriage as the "quick-fix" solution to poverty will force poor women to choose between their children or remaining in or entering abusive relationships. The author is vice president for program and public policy with the National Partnership for Women and Families, an organization that helps women meet the demands of work and family.

As you read, consider the following questions:
1. According to Rubiner, what percentage of families living in poverty were headed by single women?
2. What alternatives to marriage does Rubiner suggest welfare policy should be focusing on to improve the lives of poor women?
3. In the author's opinion, how should welfare policy be developed in response to changing family arrangements?

Excerpted from Laurie Rubiner's testimony before the House Committee on Ways and Means, Subcommittee on Human Resources, April 24, 2001.

If we are truly committed to helping people out of poverty, then our public policies should be directed at providing real supports to those who are living in poverty. Such assistance should be provided not based upon family composition but rather upon the needs of the family and the adults' willingness to follow the rules we have established for receiving aid. The mission of welfare reform should be to reduce poverty and help people achieve economic independence, not to engage in social engineering or discrimination against families that don't meet a particular ideal about family composition. Nor should welfare reform legislation be used as a vehicle to punish families who fail to conform to our individual views of what a family should or should not be. We should learn from our past welfare policy that attempts to influence family formation can backfire.

Legislation to reauthorize the Temporary Assistance for Needy Families (TANF) program must be grounded in several, central guiding principles: all eligible families in need who follow program rules must be treated fairly and have equal access to assistance; welfare policies must help all types of families move out of poverty; and welfare policies must be designed to provide a wide variety of supports that can promote strong, healthy families.

Assistance for All Eligible Families

It is essential that welfare policies are developed with a primary focus on providing assistance and supports to all eligible families in need and not just a favored few. Some have suggested that married couples should be given preferential treatment in the distribution of scarce welfare benefits, under the theory that this will encourage people to get married. Such a policy would be misguided. First, there is no conclusive evidence that links increased marriage rates to increased welfare benefits. Second, to give preference to families solely because they are comprised of a married couple with children discriminates against those who are not married, but are working hard and playing by the rules.

Consider the example of Elizabeth Jones in Katherine Boo's recent article about moving from welfare to work in the *New Yorker* Magazine. Ms. Jones followed the rules of the 1996 welfare reform law. She left welfare and got not one, but two jobs to care for her three children. She sleeps four hours a night. Even with a day job as a D.C. police officer and a night job in private security she still can't make ends meet. Meanwhile, because she can't afford child care, her school-age children are left to care for themselves after school in a rundown apartment in a dangerous D.C. neighborhood. And, while Ms. Jones may be in the "success" column of welfare recipients who have moved into financial independence, it is hard to understand how anyone after reading her story could not agree that scarce welfare resources should be used to help her get the kinds of supports that we know help families like the Joneses, such as quality affordable childcare, health insurance and transportation.

In distributing our limited resources we must begin with the reality of who is living in poverty and in need of assistance. The face of poverty in the United States is diverse:

• Nearly 6.7 million families, consisting of 23.4 million individuals, were living in poverty in 1999—half were black or Hispanic families;

• 53% were families headed by single female heads of households;

• 7% were families headed by single male heads of households, and 40% were married couples;

• 88% of single-headed households were headed by women; almost 62% of these female-headed families with children living in poverty were headed by black or Hispanic women.

While there has been important progress in reducing poverty rates, there clearly is more work to do. There are a wide range of strategies—from ensuring access to quality education and training, to job creation, to increasing Medicaid enrollment and providing affordable health care, to expansion of the Earned Income Tax Credit—that collectively can and should be pursued to help more families achieve economic security. Any serious efforts to develop sound, effective welfare policies must have as their central goal a commitment to serving all eligible families in need.

It is particularly crucial to pay special attention to the needs of families facing unique hurdles, such as families stuck at the bottom of the economic ladder, welfare clients with limited English proficiency or disabilities, and clients with multiple barriers to employment. Poverty has deepened for the poorest 20% of female-headed families and many are worse off today than they were six years ago. Recent data, for example, indicates that between 1995 and 1999 the inflation-adjusted disposable income of female-headed families with the lowest incomes actually declined by 4 percent. Many clients with limited English proficiency have been unable to get the services they need because they cannot get accurate information about their program in other languages. Many clients with disabilities have been shut out of training or job opportunities because their dis-

Is Welfare to Blame?

Conservatives have put the blame for the rise in single teenage mothers squarely on welfare. Charles Murray, for example, argued that welfare benefits, especially for black women, greatly reduce the costs of illegitimacy. Therefore, eliminating welfare benefits would be an effective policy response to the rise in out-of-wedlock births, including teenage childbearing. Yet Robert Moffitt, in his extensive review of studies on the effect of welfare on family structure, concluded that the effects are small in magnitude and could not explain the rapid rise in single-parenthood during the 1960s and early 1970s. In a more recent review of the effects of welfare on nonmarital childbearing, Moffitt pointed to the difficult methodological issues of imputing causality. He suggested that although the welfare system may increase nonmarital childbearing, its effect is small in comparison to other contributing factors, such as the availability of employed men.

Focusing specifically on black female teenagers, Greg Duncan and Saul Hoffman used data from the Panel Study of Income Dynamics (PSID) to estimate the effects of Aid to Families with Dependent Children (AFDC) benefit levels as compared with future economic opportunities on out-of-wedlock births. They found "that AFDC benefit levels have a modest but statistically insignificant positive effect on the incidence of teenage out-of-wedlock birth, whereas future economic opportunities have a larger and statistically significant negative effect." They estimated that a 25 percent increase in AFDC benefits will result in a 1 percent increase in out-of-wedlock births.

Joel F. Handler and Yeheskel Hasenfeld, *We, the Poor People*, 1997.

ability has not been assessed or adequately accommodated.

Still other welfare clients face a combination of employment barriers—limited opportunities to acquire education or build skills, unreliable childcare, mental and physical health problems, and lack of transportation—that together make it even more difficult to leave welfare and achieve some level of economic security. A research study by the University of Michigan of welfare clients in an urban Michigan county found that multiple employment barriers—such as low education, lack of job skills, lack of transportation, health problems, perceived discrimination, and domestic violence—were common: 37% of clients reported having two or three different employment barriers, 24% reported having four to six barriers, and 3% reported having 7 or more barriers. And increasingly many low-income fathers are struggling to acquire new skills and find and retain jobs. All of these clients have unique needs that require focused, targeted strategies—such as offering English as a Second Language classes, or training programs for non-traditional, higher-paying careers. Most importantly, it is critical that we do not create policies that pit different groups against each other to compete for much-needed services. Low-income mothers and low-income fathers who are underemployed or unemployed both need access to education and training—and we should take steps to make sure that both can have access to the services they need.

Coercive Policies Undermine Families

Coercive policies designed to promote certain types of family structures at the expense of others, particularly children, will do more to undermine families than strengthen them. We ought not to desecrate the ideal of marriage by "paying people to get married," nor should we endorse policies that penalize families that are most in need because they do not conform to a preferred family structure. If marriage were only about economics, and the road out of poverty were as simple as a walk down the aisle, then policies that provide financial incentives to people to get married would be appropriate. But a successful marriage is a much more complicated equation, with more than one variable, and a marriage license is not a winning lottery ticket. Kathryn Edin's study of marriage among low-income women reveals that they look for the same things the rest of us look for in a mate. Yes, they want someone with a stable income, but they also want kindness, partnership, respect, emotional support, and a good father for their children. It should come as no surprise that low-income women want the same kinds of marriages that we want for ourselves and our children and that they prefer to remain single than enter into an unstable, unsuitable, or abusive marriage.

Rather than simply promoting marriage as a "quick-fix" economic solution, we ought to be focused on helping individuals make sound, reasonable, responsible decisions about their relationships and their lives, so that if they do choose to get married the marriage will be stable and will be less likely to end in divorce. Helping to equip individuals to make the right choices ultimately can help strengthen both marriages and families. If our sole focus is on making a family look the way we want it to look, then we risk ignoring important pieces of the equation that can impact whether families grow together and get stronger or fall apart.

Most importantly, marriage should not be used as a band-aid to cure other, more complicated problems. Many clients have turned to TANF as a source of critical support as they try to address difficult problems such as domestic violence or a family health crisis. Several different research studies have found, for example, that significant percentages of welfare clients are victims of domestic violence. A study of a scientific sampling of 734 female welfare clients in Massachusetts found that 19.5% reported current physical violence and 64% reported experiencing domestic violence at some point as an adult. Similar research involving 846 female welfare clients in Passaic County, New Jersey, found that nearly 14.6% reported current physical abuse, 25% reported verbal or emotional abuse, and 57.3% reported physical abuse at some point during adulthood. Women who have been in abusive relationships and who need TANF assistance to be able to escape their abusers should not be penalized for trying to take control of their lives and create a safer and emotionally sound environment for their children. Forcing them to get married will only exacerbate their problems. To promote policies that put women, or any low-income individual, in the position of having to choose between financial support for their children or remaining in an abusive or destructive situation is wrong and not good policy. And it will do little to create the strong, healthy families that we claim to support.

Enabling Relationships

In the long term, helping to equip individuals with the skills and judgment needed to make the right decisions about their families, and effectively manage their work and family responsibilities, is the best strategy for fostering strong/healthy families, strong/healthy marriages, and strong/healthy relationships.

In crafting policies, there are a number of factors to keep in mind:

• Protections for victims of domestic violence, child abuse, or other forms of abuse. Clients should not be forced or coerced into remaining in unhealthy, abusive relationships because they are unable to receive TANF assistance. Clients who face these types of problems should be able to get TANF assistance and other supports, and they should not be excluded from certain types of benefits because they are not married. Privacy protections are essential to ensure that clients can share sensitive information without fear of putting themselves and their families at risk, but also to ensure that clients are not forced to navigate cumbersome requirements to establish that they are victims of domestic violence or other forms of abuse.

• Education and counseling on responsible decision-making and sustaining healthy relationships. Education programs, primarily targeted at youth, that focus on making responsible choices, entering into healthy relationships, and understanding the family situations that offer the best chance for children's growth and success can help clients to be informed and thoughtful about the choices they make and the consequences of those choices.

• Efforts to remove penalties to marriage—individuals should not be paid to get married, but they should not be penalized if they get married. Welfare policies should be neutral on the subject of family formation and instead target resources where they are most needed.

• Voluntary participants. Clients must not be forced to marry as a condition to receive benefits; clients must not be coerced into special "marriage incentive programs" by dangling the promise of basic benefits that are critical to their family's survival.

Supports to Help Strengthen Low-Income Families

One priority in developing new welfare policies must be to provide support and promote strong, healthy families in all their different forms. Clearly, we should support strong marriages and married couples, and remove impediments to marriage that discourage individuals who want to marry. But we ought to create these types of policies with our eyes open and not shut to the realities facing many families. Rather than focusing merely on getting individuals married regardless of whether there is a solid foundation, our focus ought to be on what it takes to make marriages work. To the extent that we want to assist low-income married couples who receive welfare, or are recent welfare leavers, we should concentrate on addressing the real problems that they face, such as removing TANF provisions that place additional burdens on married couples, and increasing the availability of transitional childcare, family and medical leave, affordable health care, and affordable housing.

But we cannot limit our support only to married couple families who represent only a portion of all families. We have to promote strong, healthy families in whatever way they are constructed. Very few would disagree that having two parents in the home working together to provide a healthy and nurturing environment can be an ideal setting for children. But it is not the reality for many children. And, given that, we cannot conclude that it is the only environment in which children can prosper and grow. We must be willing to take a variety of steps to support low-income families headed by single parents to give their children the best chance to succeed. In addition, there are many families where grandparents, other relatives, and family friends are struggling to keep families together. We ought to do everything we can to strengthen those bonds and help those families stay intact and survive.

As we craft new welfare policies, we ought not to operate in a vacuum. Targeting benefits only at married couples will leave millions of hard-working single-parent families without adequate resources, exacerbating their already difficult circumstances. The stark reality is that married couple families are on the decline. If the Congress wants to try to reverse this trend through non-punitive, non-discriminatory policies, it should do so. But those policies should not be a substitute for providing supports to the families who have immediate needs that must be met.

The most recent Census Bureau statistics reveal significant shifts in the different types of families in our country. Less than a quarter of American households—23.5%—are composed of traditional, "nuclear" families with two married parents living at home with children. The number of single-parent families is growing at a faster rate than married couple families. These numbers only confirm that family arrangements are becoming increasingly complex and the concept of what constitutes a family is changing.

It is in this context that we must develop welfare policies that are responsive to the needs of different types of families living in poverty. Our efforts should be informed by an accurate, comprehensive understanding of the families being served, and by what we have learned about policies that work and policies that do not work. We already know from history that we have to exercise care in constructing policies that may impact how families compose themselves. Some have criticized the prior Aid to Families with Dependent Children (AFDC) system because there were marriage disincentives. To the extent that the old AFDC law may have had incentives that discouraged certain types of families, we ought not to repeat those same mistakes. Nor should we penalize families now because they followed the old rules by changing those rules in the middle of the game. One lesson that we should have learned from the past is that we must proceed with caution when crafting policies that affect families when they are at their most vulnerable. If we want to move families out of poverty, then we first have to be willing to understand the reality of their lives and develop policies that enable them to become economically secure, whatever their structure. We ought not to have disincentives to marriage, but we ought not to coerce individuals into getting married either.

Marriage Is Not the Solution

Equally important, we must not endorse policies that discriminate against certain types of families, nor should we oversimplify the problems of families living in poverty. The vast majority of single-parent families receiving TANF are headed by women, and they would be affected disproportionately by any policy that relegates them to "second-class family" status. Adopting policies that have the effect of discriminating against female-headed families in favor of married couples is unfair, unwise, and unnecessary. Denying supports to the families who often are most in need not only hurts families, but also ultimately will lead to more long-term costs as these families struggle to survive.

More fundamentally, we cannot assume that the problems facing single-headed households living in poverty—whether headed by women or by men—will be solved simply by getting married. Marriage is not a panacea: there are a multitude of factors that lead to poverty in this country; we ought not to oversimplify them or ignore their complexities. If two parents are unemployed and have limited job skills, marriage alone may do little to solve that problem. In fact, such a marriage will undergo significant stress and is much more likely to dissolve. If we are committed to the goal of helping families move out of poverty, then first and foremost we have to be willing to provide concrete supports that can help make that dream a reality. A report released by the National Campaign for Jobs and Income, for example, revealed that many states have significant TANF surpluses even though many welfare clients cannot access much-needed supports like childcare. It is critical that states provide basic supports to low-income families, and make investments in important strategies like the creation of livable wage jobs, so that families can have a realistic chance of achieving economic independence. And these basic supports should not be ignored in favor of largely unproven policies—such as paying clients to get married—that may not even scratch the surface of the underlying problems that clients confront on a daily basis.

These cautionary words about marriage formation policies in the context of welfare reform are not a condemnation of marriage, or an effort to discourage individuals who want to get married. It is precisely out of respect for what the institution of marriage should be that I reject outdated notions about which people are more deserving of support, and resist efforts to use marriage as the solution to other, more complicated problems. But most importantly, I urge you not to allow a discussion about marriage to divert attention from the task at hand—adopting concrete, comprehensive policies to provide all families in need with the supports they need to make a permanent transition from welfare to economic security.

Periodical Bibliography

The following articles have been selected to supplement the diverse views presented in this chapter.

Ken Boettcher	"Welfare Reform No Success for Capitalism's Poorest Victims," *People*, December 2000.
Ronald Brownstein	"Welfare Reform Makes a Case for Boosting Welfare of Working Poor," *Los Angeles Times*, August 16, 1999.
Business Week	"From Welfare to Worsefare?" October 9, 2000.
Jason DeParle	"Bold Effort Leaves Much Unchanged for the Poor," *New York Times*, December 30, 1999.
Patricia Donovan	"The 'Illegitimacy Bonus' and State Efforts to Reduce Out-of-Wedlock Births," *Family Planning Perspectives*, March/April 1999.
Fred Gaboury	"End 'Welfare Reform' as We Know It," *People's Weekly World*, January 20, 2001.
Rudolph W. Giuliani	"The Welfare Reform Battle Isn't Over Yet," *Wall Street Journal*, February 3, 1999.
Mickey Kaus	"Workfare's Misguided Critics," *New York Times*, May 5, 1998.
June O'Neill	"Welfare Reform Worked," *Wall Street Journal*, August 1, 2001.
Frances Fox Piven	"Thompson's Easy Ride," *Nation*, February 26, 2001.
Wendell Primus	"What Next for Welfare Reform?" *Brookings Review*, Summer 2001.
Joel Schwartz	"What the Poor Need Most," *American Enterprise*, March 2001.
John C. Weicher	"Reforming Welfare: The Next Policy Debates," *Society*, January 2001.
Aimee Welch	"Welfare Reform Still Needs Work," *Insight on the News*, December 25, 2000.
Joe Wilensky	"How Have Children Fared Under Welfare Reform?," *Human Ecology*, Winter 2001.

For Further Discussion

Chapter 1

1. Kathryn Edin and Laura Lein maintain that the majority of welfare recipients they interviewed were planning to leave welfare but could not afford to take the dead-end, minimum wage jobs available to them. James L. Payne argues that welfare recipients have no incentive to give up their carefree welfare "careers," since they would have to find jobs paying more than $9.18 an hour to equal their earnings from welfare. Which author makes the more convincing argument for the reasons mothers remain on welfare? Why?

2. In their viewpoint, Michael Tanner and David B. Kopel cite several studies in support of their contention that easy access to welfare has increased unwed child-bearing and hastened the decline of the nuclear family. Michael B. Katz contends that the research linking welfare and out-of-wedlock births is flawed. Which author's use of evidence do you find more effective? Why?

Chapter 2

1. James L. Payne contends that welfare recipients who commit fraud are taking advantage of lax enforcement by welfare officials. Karen Seccombe asserts that welfare recipients engage in fraud as a survival tactic to make up for inadequate benefits. With which author do you agree most? Support your position using examples from the viewpoints.

2. John Smith argues that collecting child support in welfare cases produces no benefit to the mother or children because the money often goes to the government as reimbursement for welfare benefits. Elaine Sorensen and Ariel Halpern maintain that enforcing child support collection from "deadbeat dads" while single-mother families are on welfare ensures that families will continue to receive child support payments when they leave the welfare system. Which author's argument do you find most convincing? Why?

3. Sara Paretsky maintains that the costs of providing cash assistance to refugees will ultimately be repaid many times over in the federal income taxes they pay. Don Barnett argues that refugees are being encouraged to take advantage of every available welfare loophole, slowing their entry into the workforce and wasting taxpayers' money. How would Paretsky respond to

Barnett's contention that refugees are a drain on taxpayers? Does the fact that Paretsky is the granddaughter of a refugee affect your opinion of her argument? Explain.

Chapter 3

1. David Kelley contends that private aid will help the poor more than wasteful welfare programs will. Janet Poppendieck argues that relying on private charities ignores the root causes of poverty and is not an adequate substitute for welfare. In your opinion, would voluntary contributions to charities be enough to help the poor? Defend your position using examples from the viewpoints.

2. Do you agree with Ronald J. Sider's assessment that churches offer special strengths? Explain your answer drawing from the viewpoint and any personal experiences.

3. Peter Cove maintains that his company, America Works, has been highly successful in contracting with state governments to place welfare recipients in full-time jobs. In particular, Cove contends that 88 percent of the people in New York State placed by America Works remain off the welfare rolls three years later. Bill Berkowitz asserts that America Works has been paid more than $1 million from New York State for welfare recipients who never found jobs or who were placed in temporary positions. Which author are you more inclined to believe? Explain your answer using examples from the viewpoints.

Chapter 4

1. Charles Murray argues that the welfare system should be reformed to put more pressure on recipients to get jobs, sending the message that dependency and illegitimacy are bad and should be reduced. Jared Bernstein and Mark Greenberg contend that the welfare system must be enhanced to provide more assistance to recipients as they make the transition from welfare to work. In your opinion, will more help for welfare recipients lessen or increase their incentive to find jobs? Explain.

2. Ron Haskins contends that requiring welfare recipients to work has simultaneously reduced poverty and the welfare rolls as more and more people have taken jobs. In Randy Albelda's opinion, why should mandatory work requirements be discontinued? How would more flexibility regarding work help single mothers, according to Albelda? Which author's use of statistics do you find more effective? Why?

3. Lisa E. Oliphant argues that the welfare system should be reformed to discourage women from having children out of wedlock. What methods does she propose to accomplish this goal?
   How do Oliphant's proposals contrast with Laurie Rubiner's
   view of welfare policies? In your opinion, should the government have a say in how women conduct their personal lives?
   Defend your position, citing examples from the viewpoints.

Organizations to Contact

The editors have compiled the following list of organizations concerned with the issues debated in this book. The descriptions are derived from materials provided by the organizations. All have publications or information available for interested readers. The list was compiled on the date of publication of the present volume; the information provided here may change. Be aware that many organizations take several weeks or longer to respond to inquiries, so allow as much time as possible.

American Enterprise Institute (AEI)
1150 17th St. NW, Washington, DC 20036
(202) 862-5500 • fax: (202) 862-7177
website: www.aei.org

AEI is a conservative public policy research organization that favors limited government and free enterprise. The institute publishes the monthly magazine *American Enterprise* and the monthly *On the Issues* newsletter in addition to numerous articles, books, and reports critical of welfare.

Brookings Institution
1775 Massachusetts Ave. NW, Washington, DC 20036-2188
(202) 797-6104 • fax: (202) 797-6319
e-mail: brookinfo@brook.edu • website: www.brook.edu

The Brookings Institution is a private, nonprofit organization that conducts research on economics, education, foreign and domestic government policy, and the social sciences. Its research supports the success of welfare reform in moving former welfare recipients into the workforce. The institution publishes the quarterly *Brookings Review* and many books through its publishing division, the Brookings Institution Press.

Cato Institute
1000 Massachusetts Ave. NW, Washington, DC 20001-5403
(202) 842-0200 • fax: (202) 842-3490
e-mail: cato@cato.org • website: www.cato.org

The Cato Institute is a libertarian public policy research foundation dedicated to limiting the role of government and protecting individual liberties. The institute favors lower taxes and is skeptical about the benefits of welfare. It publishes the quarterly magazine *Regulation* and the bimonthly *Cato Policy Report*, in addition to many books and reports on the ineffectiveness of welfare programs.

Center on Urban Poverty and Social Change

Mandel School of Applied Social Sciences, Case Western Reserve University
10900 Euclid Ave., Cleveland, OH 44106-7164
(216) 368-6946 • fax: (216) 368-5158
e-mail: povertyinfo@po.cwru.edu
website: http://povertycenter.cwru.edu

The center works to address problems of persistent poverty in urban areas and attempts to understand how social and economic changes affect low-income communities. The center takes the position that welfare recipients need more government assistance in transitioning from welfare to work. It publishes several articles and reports on welfare reform including "Welfare Reform, Public Housing, and Job Accessibility" and "Employment Dynamics in the Welfare-to-Work Transition in Cuyahoga County."

Economic Policy Institute (EPI)

1660 L St. NW, Suite 1200, Washington, DC 20036
(202) 775-8810 • fax: (202) 775-0819
e-mail: epi@epinet.org • website: www.epinet.org

EPI conducts research and promotes education programs on economic policy issues, particularly the economics of poverty, unemployment, and American industry. The institute believes that government should do more to help the working poor who have been pushed off the welfare rolls as a result of welfare reform. It publishes the quarterly *EPI Journal* and the monthly *EPI News*, which details its latest research publications.

Employment Policies Institute (EPI)

1775 Pennsylvania Ave. NW, Suite 1200, Washington, DC 20006-4605
(202) 463-7650 • fax: (202) 463-7107
e-mail: epi@epionline.org • website: www.epionline.org

The institute is a nonprofit research organization that believes entry-level employment opportunities often provide the best job-training opportunities for young Americans and those seeking to move from welfare to work. EPI also maintains that a government-set minimum wage destroys these opportunities. Its publications include articles on low-wage workers and the negative effects of raising the minimum wage.

Heritage Foundation

214 Massachusetts Ave. NE, Washington, DC 20002-4999
(202) 546-4400 • fax: (202) 546-8328
e-mail: info@heritage.org • website: www.heritage.org

The Heritage Foundation is a conservative think tank that promotes public policy based on limited government and individual freedom. The foundation advocates serious reform of the welfare system in such areas as controlling rising welfare costs and reducing out-of-wedlock births. It publishes numerous policy papers on welfare including "Means-Tested Welfare Spending: Past and Future Growth" and "The Federal and State Governments, Welfare and Marriage Issues," in addition to the bimonthly journal *Policy Review*.

Institute for Women's Policy Research (IWPR)

1707 L St. NW, Suite 750, Washington, DC 20036
(202) 785-5100
e-mail: iwpr@iwpr.org • website: www.iwpr.org

IWPR is a research organization working to encourage the debate on welfare, poverty, and other public policy issues of importance to women and their families. The institute takes the position that poor women need more education and job training if welfare reform is to succeed. Its reports on welfare include "Working First but Working Poor: The Need for Education and Training Following Welfare Reform," and "The Effects of Welfare Reform on Housing Stability and Homelessness: Current Research Findings, Legislation, and Programs."

National Center for Children in Poverty (NCCP)

Mailman School of Public Health, Columbia University
154 Haven Ave., New York, NY 10032
(212) 304-7100 • fax: (212) 544-4200
e-mail: nccp@columbia.edu
website: http://cpmcnet.columbia.edu

NCCP promotes strategies to prevent child poverty and improve the lives of low-income children and their families. The center believes that both the public and private sectors have a role to play in reducing child poverty. It publishes the quarterly newsletter *News & Issues*, covering topics related to welfare research. NCCP also publishes several articles on welfare reform.

NOW Legal Defense and Education Fund

395 Hudson St., New York, NY 10014
(212) 925-6635 • fax: (212) 226-1066
e-mail: lir@nowldef.org • website: www.nowldef.org

The fund is the educational and litigating arm of the National Organization for Women. It provides legal assistance to women and employs education and community-based projects to combat discrimination based on gender. The fund is against government efforts to control the reproductive rights of welfare recipients. It publishes many reports on welfare such as "What Congress Didn't Tell You: A State-by-State Guide to the Welfare Law's Hidden Reproductive Rights Agenda."

Progressive Policy Institute (PPI)
600 Pennsylvania Ave. SE, Suite 400, Washington, DC 20003
(202) 547-0001 • fax: (202) 544-5014
website: www.ppionline.org

PPI is a research and education institute working to promote progressive politics in America. The institute supports more government intervention to help welfare recipients find adequate employment, but it is critical of conservative efforts to promote marriage as a path out of poverty for single mothers. PPI publishes the *New Dem Daily*, an online newsletter, and policy reports on poverty, marriage, and welfare.

Urban Institute
2100 M St. NW, Washington, DC 20037
(202) 833-7200
e-mail: paffairs@ui.urban.org • website: www.urban.org

The Urban Institute conducts nonpartisan research to improve government decision making and increase citizens' awareness concerning public policy issues like welfare reform and the low-wage labor market. The institute's reports on welfare include "Poor Dads Who Don't Pay Child Support: Deadbeats or Disadvantaged?" and "How Are Families That Left Welfare Doing? A Comparison of Early and Recent Welfare Leavers."

Welfare Policy Center of the Hudson Institute (WPC)
5395 Emerson Way, Indianapolis, IN 46226
(317) 549-4102 • fax: (317) 545-9639
website: www.welfarereformer.org

WPC conducts research on welfare reform programs from around the country in order to help governments determine which reforms are the most effective. The center is a branch of the Hudson Institute, a conservative think tank, and maintains that work-based welfare reforms are the best way to reduce the welfare rolls and the costs of the welfare state. WPC publishes books and articles on welfare reform including *Transforming Charity* and *Ending Dependency: Lessons from Welfare Reform in the USA*.

Bibliography of Books

Mimi Abramovitz   *Regulating the Lives of Women: Social Welfare Policy from Colonial Times to the Present.* Boston: South End Press, 1996.

Mimi Abramovitz   *Under Attack, Fighting Back: Women and Welfare in the United States.* New York: Monthly Review Press, 1996.

A.B. Atkinson   *The Economic Consequences of Rolling Back the Welfare State.* Cambridge, MA: MIT Press, 1999.

Dan Bloom   *Welfare Time Limits: An Interim Report Card.* New York: Manpower Demonstration Research, 1999.

Michael K. Brown   *Race, Money, and the American Welfare State.* Ithaca, NY: Cornell University Press, 1999.

Anne Marie Cammisa   *From Rhetoric to Reform? Welfare Policy in American Politics.* Boulder, CO: Westview Press, 1998.

David E. Card and Rebecca M. Blank, eds.   *Finding Jobs: Work and Welfare Reform.* New York: Russell Sage Foundation, 2000.

Nancy E. Dowd   *In Defense of Single-Parent Families.* New York: New York University Press, 1997.

Peter Edelman   *Searching for America's Heart: RFK and the Renewal of Hope.* Boston: Houghton Mifflin, 2001.

Kathryn Edin   *Single Mothers and Absent Fathers: The Possibilities and Limits of Child Support Policy.* Piscataway, NJ: Center for Urban Policy Research, 1994.

Kathryn Edin and Laura Lein   *Making Ends Meet: How Single Mothers Survive Welfare and Low-Wage Work.* New York: Russell Sage Foundation, 1997.

Timothy J. Gaffaney   *Freedom for the Poor: Welfare and the Foundations of Democratic Citizenship.* Boulder, CO: Westview Press, 2000.

Irwin Garfinkel et al., eds.   *Fathers Under Fire: The Revolution in Child Support Enforcement.* New York: Russell Sage Foundation, 1998.

Martin Gilens   *Why Americans Hate Welfare: Race, Media, and the Politics of Antipoverty Policy.* Chicago: University of Chicago Press, 1999.

Joel F. Handler and Yeheskel Hasenfeld   *We the Poor People: Work, Poverty, and Welfare.* New Haven, CT: Yale University Press, 1997.

| John E. Hansan and Robert Morris, eds. | *Welfare Reform, 1996–2000.* Westport, CT: Auburn House, 1999. |

Christopher Howard — *The Hidden Welfare State: Tax Expenditures and Social Policy in the United States.* Princeton, NJ: Princeton University Press, 1997.

Earl S. Johnson, Ann Levine, and Fred C. Doolittle — *Fathers' Fair Share: Helping Poor Men Manage Child Support and Fatherhood.* New York: Russell Sage Foundation, 1999.

Jyl J. Josephson — *Gender, Families, and State: Child Support Policy in the United States.* Lanham, MD: Rowman & Littlefield, 1997.

David Kelley — *A Life of One's Own: Individual Rights and the Welfare State.* Washington, DC: Cato Institute, 1998.

Robert C. Lieberman — *Shifting the Color Line: Race and the American Welfare State.* Cambridge, MA: Harvard University Press, 1998.

Joyce M. Mercier, Steven B. Garasky, and Mack C. Shelley II, eds. — *Redefining Family Policy: Implications for the 21st Century.* Ames: Iowa State University Press, 2000.

Gwendolyn Mink — *Welfare's End.* Ithaca, NY: Cornell University Press, 1998.

Ann Morse et al. — *America's Newcomers: Mending the Safety Net for Immigrants.* Denver: National Conference of State Legislatures, 1998.

Charles Noble — *Welfare as We Knew It: A Political History of the American Welfare State.* New York: Oxford University Press, 1997.

James L. Payne — *Overcoming Welfare: Expecting More from the Poor—and from Ourselves.* New York: BasicBooks, 1998.

Edmund S. Phelps — *Rewarding Work: How to Restore Participation and Support to Free Enterprise.* Cambridge, MA: Harvard University Press, 1997.

Janet Poppendieck — *Sweet Charity? Emergency Food and the End of Entitlement.* New York: Viking, 1998.

Pierre Rosanvallon — *The New Social Question: Rethinking the Welfare State.* Princeton, NJ: Princeton University Press, 2000.

Peter H. Rossi — *Feeding the Poor: Assessing Federal Food Aid.* Washington, DC: AEI Press, 1998.

Sanford F. Schram and Samuel H. Beer, eds. — *Welfare Reform: A Race to the Bottom?* Washington, DC: Woodrow Wilson Center Press, 1999.

Karen Seccombe — *"So You Think I Drive a Cadillac?" Welfare Recipients' Perspectives on the System and Its Reform.* Boston: Allyn and Bacon, 1999.

Robert M. Solow — *Work and Welfare.* Princeton, NJ: Princeton University Press, 1998.

Michael Tanner — *The End of Welfare: Fighting Poverty in the Civil Society.* Washington, DC: Cato Institute, 1996.

Jack Tweedie et al. — *Meeting the Challenges of Welfare Reform: Programs with Promise.* Denver: National Conference of State Legislatures, 1998.

David Wagner — *What's Love Got to Do with It? A Critical Look at American Charity.* New York: New Press, 2000.

Maureen Waller and Robert Plotnick — *Child Support and Low-Income Families: Perceptions, Practices, and Policy.* San Francisco: Public Policy Institute of California, 1999.

David Zucchino — *Myth of the Welfare Queen: A Pulitzer Prize–Winning Journalist's Portrait of Women on the Line.* New York: Scribner, 1997.

Index

Osborn, David, 145
out-of-wedlock births
  as percentage of all births, 201
  social disapproval reduces, 26–27
  trends in, 39
  welfare causes increase in, 38–44
    con, 45–50, 210
  welfare policies should discourage,
    197–206
Ozawa, Martha, 43

Panel Study of Income Dynamics, 31,
  210
Paretsky, Sara, 88
Parker, Star, 59
paternity
  establishing, for child support
    enforcement, 73–75
Payne, James L., 20, 55, 110
Pearce, Diana, 36
Perkins, Frances, 43
Perry, Cecilia, 151
Personal Responsibility and Work
  Opportunity Reconciliation Act
  (PRWORA), 73–74, 90, 120, 150,
  162, 163
  considerations in reauthorization of,
    174–76
  findings of, 189
Picchi, Bernard, 152
Pizarro, Rosemarie, 53
Plotnick, Robert, 43
Ponnuru, Ramesh, 14
Poppendieck, Janet, 117
Postrel, Virginia, 15
poverty
  Census Bureau measurement of, 182,
    185
  characteristics of individuals in, 209
  child, declines in, 183
  economic factors vs. single-parent
    families as cause of, 131
  is caused by behavioral problems,
    114
  measurement of, does not include in-
    kind federal benefits, 183
  private charity normalizes, 120–22
  reduction of, should be goal of
    welfare reform, 175
  work requirements and government
    subsidies will reduce, 180–87
poverty rate
  War on Poverty and, 105–106
pregnancy, teen
  link with welfare dependence, 200
  is insignificant, 210
  prevention programs, 200–201
  welfare reform and, 205

Private Sector Initiative Program, 96
privatization of welfare
  benefits recipients, 139–48
  con, 149–59
Proxmire, William, 155
psychological disorders
  link with out-of-wedlock births,
    40–41

Quayle, Dan, 39

race
  welfare as code word for, 50
Reagan, Ronald, 194
Rector, Robert, 46, 47
Reed, Lawrence W., 158
Refugee Act of 1980, 96, 101
refugee resettlement agencies
  government funding of, 96–97
refugees
  deserve welfare assistance from
    government, 88–92
    con, 93–102
  health services for, 95
  receiving assistance, 99
  U.S. admissions of, 97
Reinert, Jennifer, 154
religious organizations
  can reduce poverty, 127–38
Rosen, Miriam, 155–56
Rosenzweig, Marl, 43
Rubiner, Laurie, 207

Sagan, Carl, 133
Santorum, Rick, 47
Sawicky, Max, 158
Searching for America's Heart (Peter
  Edelman), 18
Seccombe, Karen, 61, 106
Sexton, Joe, 53
Shalala, Donna, 96
Shapiro, Isaac, 36
Sherman, Amy, 134, 165, 167
Sider, Ronald J., 127
Smith, Cheryl, 97
Smith, John, 78
social capital
  lack of, in low-wage jobs, 35
social disapproval
  as deterrent to harmful behavior, 26
Social Security Act of 1935, 194
  Title IV-D of, 71
Social Security Administration (SSA)
  fraud control in, 58–59
Solomon, Gerald, 49
Sorensen, Elaine, 69
Spalter-Roth, Roberta, 34
states